GROWING INDOORS

Marshall Cavendish
London & Sydney

PICTURE CREDITS
A - Z Botanical Collection: 52/3
Amsterdam Bruys: 35
P. Ayres: 12
Steve Bicknell: 10, 22, 29, 30, 31, 35, 54, 65, 71, 92, 94, 97
A. Boarder: 115
Michael Boys: 19, 75, 89, 110
Pat Brindley: 55
Camera Press: 6/7
P. Chapman: 118
R. J. Corbin: 119
Paul Forrester: 39, 57, 59, 86, 87, 91, 100, 106, 107
Geoffrey Frosh: 80
P. Hunt: 114
G. Hyde: 98
D. Joyce: 85
Natural History Photographic Agency: 40
M. Nimmo: 116
D. Smith: 26
H. Smith: 9, 47(B), 58, 78, 81, 82, 83, 102
V & A Plantiques: 29

Edited by Susan Conder

Published by Marshall Cavendish Books Limited
58 Old Compton Street
London W1V 5PA

First printing 1979
This printing 1981

Printed in Hong Kong

ISBN 0 85685 485 9

INTRODUCTION

Few homes today are without plants as decoration in one form or another, whether it's just simple bulb at springtime or a complex display designed to bring year round interest to a room. However, unlike other decorations, houseplants require a fair amount of attention in order to ensure that they will remain healthy and hence make an attractive addition to the home.

Growing Indoors sets out the simple rules for houseplant success. It explains how a plant 'works' so that you can gain an insight into its requirements in the artificial environment of the home, then traces each of the steps involved in keeping and maintaining a healthy plant. From the initial stages of buying and siting right through to the more complex aspects of propagation, it covers in detail all aspects of plant maintenance. Specialities are included too – bottle gardens, bonsai and hydroponics are all discussed and fully illustrated both in colour and with step-by-step diagrams for the more difficult procedures.

A second section takes the form of a comprehensively illustrated dictionary. Divided into five major categories of houseplants – foliage and flowering plants, bulbs, ferns and cacti – it lists information on over 130 of the most popular varieties available today.

In a clear concise style and fully illustrated throughout *Growing Indoors* provides all the practical information for healthy and successful indoor plants.

CONTENTS

INTRODUCTION

The wide variety of plants available today from florists, nurseries and even department stores make selection confusing to say the least. Plants with brightly coloured foliage of flowers, or with more subtle attractions such as variegated or highly sculptured leaves; plants of every possible shape and size, all presented shoulder-to-shoulder on display.

Although we have come to expect such a wide range of choice, and a tropical houseplant in a shop window seems no more unusual than bananas or pineapples at the greengrocer, this has not always been the case. For although the history of indoor plants goes back over many centuries, it is only in the last hundred years or so that the average person could take pleasure in buying and growing them.

Plants have long been collected and admired for a variety of reasons. Besides their medicinal qualities, their inherent beauty, rarity and consequent monetary value have encouraged the transporting of plants from one part of the world to another. For example, during the early part of the 17th century, at the height of tulip mania in Holland, a single bulb from Turkey was sold for the value of over ten acres of land and fortunes were made and lost dealing in tulip bulbs.

Until mid-Victorian times, the collecting of indoor plants tended to be the province of the very wealthy. The later 17th century saw collecting orange trees as the fashionable pursuit. More than 150 varieties were cultivated, but as special glass houses, or orangeries, as well as a constant supply of heat were needed to over-winter these tender subjects, it was the prerogative of the very wealthy.

By the middle of the 19th century, however, a number of social and economic changes had occurred which made collecting and displaying indoor plants more popular than it had ever been before or has been up to the present day. In England, the Industrial Revolution had, as one result, the emergence of a large and prosperous middle class, with money to spend and an inclination to spend it. Around the same period, the repeal of the glass tax, which had previously kept the use of glass in construction to a minimum, combined with the technical discoveries enabling the production of cheap glass on a large scale, resulted in the almost overnight mushrooming of private, domestic greenhouses and conservatories — no longer the province of the upper class alone, but a symbol of the widespread and newfound prosperity.

The Victorians were collectors at heart and indoor plants were no exception. The invention of the Wardian case earlier in the century had revolutionized plant collecting in far and distant countries. The case, really a glass and metal or wood airtight terrarium, allowed seeds and plants to survive the rigours of long overland travels and dangerous sea voyages to England. Before the advent of this case, most of the plants collected in tropical and subtropical regions arrived in England dead, if they arrived at all. In a storm at sea, containers full of plants were often jettisoned first and even if they remained on deck, contact with salt spray was enough to destroy the majority of them. If properly packed, the Wardian case assured a 90 per cent survival rate and the number of new tender plants arriving yearly was overwhelming. Nurseries and Botanical Gardens sent their own expeditions to the wilds of China, Japan, India, Africa and South America to discover and send back to England new plants. In addition, missionaries, the military forces and even diplomatic personnel throughout the world became sources of new material.

It was during this period that ferns reached the height of popularity. Both indoor and hardy types, from all parts of the world, were extensively collected. Most ferns thrive in the shade and the dimly lit interiors of Victorian parlours and sitting rooms suited them admirably. Hedgerows and woods were stripped as collectors searched for more and more curious specimens. The Victorians, as a whole, were intrigued by the out-of-the-ordinary, odd and bizarre, whatever the subject. Hence Venus-fly-trap plants, which trapped and consumed insects, incredibly enormous Amazonian water lilies and ferns with forked, double or otherwise distorted fronds were highly valued. Some of these newly introduced plant oddities needed very special growing conditions and the Wardian case reappeared, this time as a permanent household fixture in which difficult specimens could be grown. Large or small, highly ornate or quite plain, the Wardian case allowed plants needing a high level of humidity to co-exist in the same room as the everpresent aspidistra, or cast-iron plant, beloved by the Victorians for its ability to survive almost any growing conditions.

As fashions changed so too did the plant varieties. Although in the early 20th century indoor plants were not so popular, certain varieties came to the fore. In the 'twenties and 'thirties, for example, cacti and succulents were the favourites. However, it was in the 'forties that a now eminent English nurseryman coined the term 'houseplant' and started what has developed into something of a revolution in the world of potted plants.

In contrast to the late 19th century, there are very few new plants to be discovered in the wild today which would make first-class indoor subjects. In spite of this, new plants are constantly being put on the market. Plant breeders are now relying on a combination of scientific knowledge and skills and chance mutation to supply them with new plants, rather than sending out expensive and risky plant-hunting expeditions.

The modern, self-branching, brightly-coloured poinsettia, *Euphorbia mikkelrochford*, is a prime

The Victorians were very fond of Wardian cases such as this one. Inside a Wardian case, the atmospheric moisture and purity can be controlled; this allows for the cultivation of very tender species of ferns in an otherwise unsuitable environment. Many of the Victorian Wardian cases were quite decorative in themselves, and some were highly embellished.

example. Always a popular plant, the Christmas trade in poinsettias has been revolutionized by the use of modern growth-depressant chemicals, which ensure that the plants are the right size and in flower at the right time. A few years ago, an enormous stock plant of poinsettia arrived in England from America. It was noticed, almost accidentally, that this stock plant had the ability to produce numerous growing shoots in the axils of the lower leaves if the growing tip was removed. Normally, poinsettias produce only one new shoot where the leaf joins the stem, immediately below the pinched-out growing tip. Because of this horticultural quirk, all poinsettias propagated from this stock plant have five or six colourful flowering bracts, instead of one or two,

and a more attractive and marketable plant has resulted.

However, modern developments have not always had beneficial effects. Hardy plants, such as honeysuckle, paeony, mahonia and berberis, once recommended as houseplants, have now been eliminated as suitable subjects due to the advent of central heating. In addition, some plants which are first-class indoor subjects are slow to propagate commercially and modern nurseries tend to shy away from them. Tragically, the hardy stalwart of the Victorian era, the Aspidistra, has been foremost among the victims. It takes such a long time to produce a marketable plant that sadly it is available today only sporadically and at a high price.

BASIC NEEDS

For many people successful indoor growing appears largely a matter of chance. However, there is an art even a science to raising houseplants and although achieving perfection depends on a fanatic commitment to creating the correct environment, the more you know about how a plant works and its origins, the more likely you will know how to meet its needs.

Very few houseplants today originate from the world's temperate zones. As they actually evolved to succeed in the temperatures outdoors, they just do not do well in the modern, centrally-heated home. They also have a natural dormancy period in the winter months which mean that they will shed their leaves with the advent of cold weather. As houseplants are required to be displayed all year round, a plant with bare branches six months of the year is far from ideal. Ivy, and its near relative, *Fatsia*, are the main exceptions to this rule. However, they do require conditions indoors which resemble those outside as much as possible. Cool airy rooms, preferably without central heating and a spell out doors in summer are best.

Occasionally, evergreen shrubs from Mediterranean regions are attempted as indoor plants; bay, often in a clipped form, myrtle and rosemary are examples. Being evergreen, they remain attractive all year round, but the problem of excessive heat and a dry atmosphere still remains. Although Mediterranean summers are hot, dry and sunny, the winters are cool and wet and plants from this region tend to drop their leaves if confronted with unnaturally warm termperatures. The frost-free greenhouse or conservatory is much more suitable for them, or even outdoors if the site is a moderately sheltered one.

Odd as it may first seem, a large number of indoor plants are tropical or sub-tropical in origin. The

While a cool light position will suit most of these plants, because of their original environment, cryptanthus and aglaonema (front left) require warmth and Fatsia japonica (back right) prefers a cool, shady situation.

Amazon basin in South America, the Central American mainland, the Congo basin in Africa and the Indo-Malayan area of Asia have been rich sources of indoor plants. This is because the temperature and light intensity inside a house most resembles that of a tropical rain forest. The relatively constant warmth which is so harmful to plants of the temperate region is positively beneficial to the cultivation of tropical plants. Although the amount of sunlight at the tree canopy level of tropical jungles is high, very little of it reaches the forest floor. Plants growing at ground level in dense tropical forests have adapted themselves admirably to making the most of the small amount of filtered sunlight that actually penetrates the dense foliage. As a rule they are broad-leaved evergreens, with a large amount of leaf surface to make use of every bit of sunlight available. This ability serves them well in the artifical environment of a sitting room or hall where there is a very limited amount of sunlight.

Because of the continually high level of humidity present in their natural environment, leaves of tropical rain-forest plants have evolved in such a way as to be able to shed water quickly. They tend to be oval or elliptical in shape, with a smooth, shiny upper surface and an elongated end point known as a drip tip. The curious perforations in the leaves of the Swiss cheese plant are thought to be yet another method of quickly shedding excess water. While all of these qualities are functional, they make for very attractive foliage as well. Although the temperature and light intensity in an average heated room suit these plants, the atmospheric moisture which exists in a tropical rain forest is obviously lacking. The dedicated grower will try to reproduce this humidity albeit in a small way, by spraying the leaves frequently with a mist sprayer or growing the plants on a tray filled with pebbles and water so that the continual evaporation makes the air humid immediately around the plants.

At the other end of the spectrum, plants from very dry environments also make their way into shops and sitting rooms as easy-to-care-for subjects. Although it is not really possible to recreate the intensity of the sunlight in their original environment, they are able to adapt to the reduced amount of light near a relatively sunny window. Being used to long periods of drought, hot summers and cold winters, they are quite tough and will survive in a wide range of temperatures. Cacti and many other succulents originate in arid environments, where their ability to store water is essential for survival. Spines are a way of protecting the plant from browsing and grazing animals during the summer months when little else is available. *Euphorbia fulgens*, crown of thorns, is a fine example. Some euphorbias have even developed a milky sap which can be unpleasant and is, in some cases, poisonous to animals.

The leaves on these plants, in many cases, have disappeared and the usual leaf functions are carried out by the stem. The lack of leaf surface thus reduces the transpiration rate and enables the plant to withstand the rigours of desert and semi-desert conditions.

In contrast, many South African plants, such as clivias and hippeastrums, have evolved a different method of storing food — in their bulbs. During the long hot summers of their environment, they remain dormant, but it only takes the first autumn rains to activate the production of food and the glorious flowering of these plants.

Light and shade

Plants need light to manufacture the sugars and starches which supply them with the energy to live, grow and reproduce. During this process, called

Many South African plants, such as clivias, store water in their bulbs or swollen roots for use during periods of drought.

12

photosynthesis, the plant uses the chlorophyll contained in the green pigment of the leaves to harness the energy in sunlight and turn carbon dioxide and water into starch and sugar. If there is insufficient light, a reduction in the amount of chlorophyll in the plant will result and the plant will be permanently weakened. It is for this reason that variegated plants tend to be weaker than their all-green counterparts; containing less chlorophyll, they manufacture less food. Likewise, they need plenty of sunlight to thrive and display their variegation fully.

Although light is necessary for a plant to live, it does not follow that the more light given, the better. The optimum amount of light needed varies enormously from plant to plant and also from season to season. It changes according to temperature and soil conditions and periods of growth and rest. Ideally, the conditions in which a plant grows in nature should be reproduced as closely as possible.

Plants respond not only to the amount of light available, but the relationship between periods of light and darkness, ie day and night. Chrysanthemums, for example, will only flower when the hours of daylight are shorter than a critical period (in this case 12 hours); many autumn-flowering species have similar requirements and are called 'short day plants'. 'Long day plants', such as evening primrose, iris and rudbeckia, will only flower if the period of light exceeds a critical amount every day. A third category, called day-neutral-plants, will flower over a wide range of light conditions.

As many indoor plants are grown for their flowers, an elementary knowledge of their light needs will result in larger and longer floral displays and a generally healthier plant.

The source of light can also have an enormous effect on the shape and attractiveness of a plant. Leaves, stems and flowers tend to grow towards a light source; this movement is called phototropism. Pot plants grown on a windowsill and not turned regularly will eventually become one-sided, each leaf facing the window in an attempt to absorb the maximum amount of light. Likewise, if the source of light is far away and weak, a plant will become drawn and spindly in its attempt to reach the light source.

Temperature

There is no one ideal temperature for all indoor plants; the optimum temperature varies enormously, depending on the natural habitat of a particular plant, its seasonal needs and even its daily needs. Perhaps the one single rule which is applicable to all indoor plants is that sudden changes of temperature should be avoided. Plants, like cold-blooded animals, tend to take on the temperature of the surrounding

environment and a sudden drop or rise can lead to wilting, leaf-drop, permanent damage and eventual death. For this reason, rooms which are heated sporadically, perhaps in the evenings, make for more difficult growing conditions than those which are kept evenly frost-free. Gas heat also presents problems; certain plants, such as begonias will simply fail to survive in the presence of gas and it is best to accept the limitation and select plants for their tolerance of gas, rather than fight a doomed battle which will sooner or later be lost.

As with light requirements, a knowledge of the original habitat is indispensable for the proper cultivation of a plant. Those from the temperate zone, for example, benefit from a gradual drop in temperature at night. This allows for a natural resting period; otherwise, all the food and energy which has been manufactured and stored during the day will be expended at night and little will be left for further growth and flowering. Tropical plants, on the other hand, resent changes in night-time temperature as conditions in their natural habitat remain relatively constant. Their period of dormancy is induced by the witholding of water during winter, while still maintaining a relatively high temperature.

Up to a certain point, the higher the temperature, the faster the rate of growth, respiration (the process by which food is broken down and energy expended) and transpiration (the process of losing water in the form of vapour from the leaf surfaces). Above a critical point, which again varies from plant to plant, all of these life processes are slowed down and the excessive heat can result in physical damage and even death.

At the other end of the scale, tolerance of cold also varies enormously. Tropical plants have a low tolerance, and even temperatures well above freezing can be fatal. Plants from the temperate zone can tolerate quite low temperatures and alpine plants, used to the rigours of a mountainous environment, lower still. It is not merely a question of tolerance, but of necessity. Periods of extreme cold allow such plants to rest and enable them to respond to the ensuing warmth of spring with renewed growth and vigour. Biennial plants will not form flowers until they have been exposed to a period of cold and seeds of many plants will not germinate unless they have been exposed to a period of very cold, even freezing, weather.

Finally, temperature should never be considered as an isolated factor. The interaction between temperature, light and water is a constantly changing one and an ideal temperature in humid conditions may be much too high for the same plant when grown in a dry atmosphere. It is really only by process of trial and error that optimum conditions are achieved.

13

Water

Plants, like people, are composed by volume largely of water. It is water pressure which gives a plant its rigidity and wilting is a sign that there is insufficient water present in the plant. Besides keeping a plant upright, water is used for general maintenance and growth. Although a very few plants, some orchids, for example, can get their water directly from water vapour in the air, most rely on absorbing rainwater from the soil by means of their roots.

Once water has been taken up by the roots, it is carried to the above-ground portion of the plant, where a large proportion is lost through evaporation from the leaves into the air. This process of losing water through evaporation is continual and it is when the rate of evaporation exceeds the rate at which water is taken into the roots that wilting occurs. The evaporation loss depends on many factors. The higher the temperature and light intensity, exposure to draughts and very dry atmospheric conditions all increase the rate of evaporation. Plants growing in environments where there is a high rate of water loss have developed in a way to overcome this problem. For example, plants with very waxy or hairy leaves or those with tough leathery leaves, lose less water than those with thin delicate leaves, and should be grown in a dry atmosphere.

Getting the right amount of water, both soil and atmospheric, to a plant at the correct time can be quite difficult. More indoor plants die from over-watering than any other cause and there are few hard and fast rules which are applicable to all indoor plants. *Cyperus* and *Acorus*, for example, are best grown with their roots actually submerged in water, as they are waterside plants whereas the roots of most other indoor plants would simply rot if grown in similar conditions. Again, the best guide is a thorough knowledge of a plant's original environment.

With indoor plants, it is not simply a question of the amount of water necessary, but the pattern of watering as well. Plants have adapted themselves over many years to the annual pattern of rainfall in their native habitat and this should be recreated as closely as possible in the artificial indoor environment. Desert plants, such as cacti and other succulents, are used to very long periods of drought followed by short rainy seasons and their wide-spreading shallow roots enable them to absorb as much rain as possible, even from the lightest shower. Alternatively, some desert plants have enormously long tap-roots which grow downwards until they find the water table. The succulent stems and leaves of desert plants operate in much the same way as a camel's hump, storing water and releasing it slowly over a long period. Giving such plants an even, steady supply of water is not a kindness but a certain method of killing them inadvertently.

Soils and feeding

As a growing medium, soil has a twofold purpose: it gives a plant a firm base in which to anchor itself and supplies a plant with the essential nutrients, air and water. The larger roots a plant sends into the soil tend to serve as anchoring roots, while minute root hairs do most of the absorption of water, in which are dissolved various minerals, compounds and trace elements. Unless a plant is hydrophytic, that is a plant which normally grows in water and has leaves and roots specially adapted to absorb oxygen from the surrounding water, the presence of air between and around the individual particles of soil is of primary importance. In a good, free-draining potting compost there are many tiny pockets of air; in water-logged soil, these spaces are filled with water. As a result, the roots cannot breathe and the plant drowns. In addition, the lack of air also kills the beneficial bacteria and a sour, acid soil results.

Water and soil are further interrelated by the fact that not all the water in the soil is available to a plant. Soil holds water in tension, and the lower the water content the greater the tension with which the water is held. This means that the roots will have little trouble in absorbing water from a throughly damp compost, but the drier it becomes, the harder it is to extract the remaining water.

When a plant grows in its natural environment, the nutrients it removes from the soil are constantly being replaced in the form of dead vegetable and animal matter which decay and are returned to the soil. In the forest, the fallen leaves and debris establish a balance between nutrients taken away and nutrients returned. The opposite is true for pot plants. They are required to live, and indeed thrive, in a very small quantity of soil from which all nutrients are removed and none returned naturally. For this reason, the initial composition of the growing medium is of the utmost importance, as even the most minor imbalance can prove fatal. Coupled with this is the need to replace nutrients artificially in exactly the right quantity so that the plant does not starve or grow too weak and lush through over feeding.

Garden soil, however good for outdoor plants, is not suitable for use with indoor plants. It is highly unlikely that the texture and chemical composition would come up to the rigorous standards required for an indoor growing medium. Moreover, a garden soil contains innumerable weed seeds, as well as bacteria and other soil organisms which may be relatively

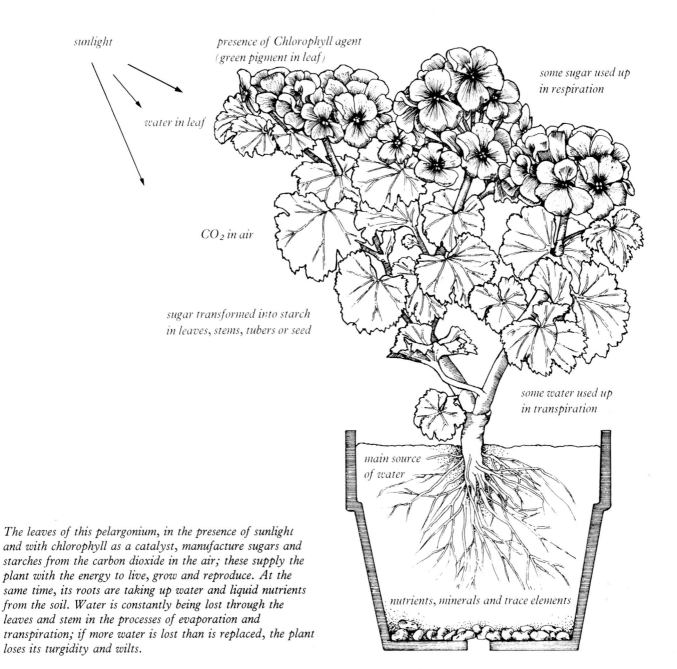

sunlight

*presence of Chlorophyll agent
(green pigment in leaf)*

*some sugar used up
in respiration*

water in leaf

CO₂ in air

*sugar transformed into starch
in leaves, stems, tubers or seed*

*some water used up
in transpiration*

*main source
of water*

nutrients, minerals and trace elements

*The leaves of this pelargonium, in the presence of sunlight
and with chlorophyll as a catalyst, manufacture sugars and
starches from the carbon dioxide in the air; these supply the
plant with the energy to live, grow and reproduce. At the
same time, its roots are taking up water and liquid nutrients
from the soil. Water is constantly being lost through the
leaves and stem in the processes of evaporation and
transpiration; if more water is lost than is replaced, the plant
loses its turgidity and wilts.*

harmless outdoors but which will thrive and cause absolute havoc indoors. A good, open loamy soil can, however, be used as the base of a potting compost if it is partially sterilized by steaming it for twenty minutes at a temperature of 93 °C (200 °F). This is hot enough to kill weed seeds and harmful bacteria, but leaves the beneficial bacteria unharmed. Special soil sterilizing units are available commercially, but it is not really worth the expense unless large quantities of soil are involved. The sterilized loam is then mixed with peat or leafmould and fertilizers according to one of several formulae.

Standardized ready-mixed composts for indoor plants are well worth the initial expense as all the guesswork has been removed and they are virtually risk-free. John Innes composts are available in three recipes, each suitable for a particular type of plant.

John Innes no. 1 is best for slow-growing plants, newly-rooted cuttings and cacti and succulents as it contains a relatively low amount of nutrients. John Innes no. 2 contains twice as much fertilizer and is probably the best all-purpose compost, while John Innes no. 3 is good for quick-growing plants, as it contains the greatest concentration of fertilizer. These three formulae, with occasional modifications, should meet the needs of most indoor plants.

LIVING WITH PLANTS

Although there are no rules guaranteeing house-plant success, there are general guidelines starting with initial selection which, if followed, can ensure a healthy and attractive display of indoor plants.

The eventual purchaser may feel that the plant's past life in the nursery is no concern of his. However, the skillful rearing of a plant before it reaches the display counter is the first factor which determines whether or not the plant will do well once purchased. Feeble plants which have been badly raised will almost invariably remain feeble. If you know a reputable grower, he is the man from whom to buy your plants. Even if the plants are slightly more expensive, it will be well worth it in the long run.

If, on the other hand, you do not have the good fortune of knowing such a grower, the next best thing is to get your plants from a reliable and under-standing retailer. Many a plant has left the grower in the peak of health, only to pine away in some draughty corner or perched on a high, inaccessible shelf in a store, getting little or no water.

The sort of plant to look for is one that is crisp, fresh and with an obvious air of good health about it. Avoid plants which have a battered appearance or equally battered wrappings around them, ostensibly to protect the plant. This paper frequently conceals

When buying poinsettias, closely inspect the tiny flower buds in the centre of the bracts; select a plant with these buds still closed to ensure a long period of floral display.

defects lower down the stem of the plant in question. The efficient grower would never dream of sending out delicate plants without the protective covering of a paper sleeve, but the plants must never remain in these covers for a moment longer than is necessary. The sensible retailer removes these covers as soon as the plants arrive so the plants get plenty of fresh air and the customers can clearly see what they are purchasing.

When selecting a plant try to avoid those with slimy pots, dirty labels or no labels at all, brown or yellow leaves or disfigured growth. Care and cultivation tags attached to the plant are seldom very explicit, largely because of their size, but they do give some guidance about the needs of a particular plant. They will usually indicate what sort of light and temperature conditions the plant needs and also its water requirements.

Although the timing is not as critical with foliage plants, it is most important to buy flowering plants at the right stage of development. Azaleas, for example, should not be bought if their flowers are all fully open or if the flower buds are too tightly shut. An azalea in full bloom will very quickly be past its best; buds which are too tightly closed may never open satisfactorily. The best plants are those which have a reasonable number of flowers fully open and plenty of buds showing colour. Chrysanthemums, on the other hand, should be bought with flowers well open or the buds may turn black and be a total disappointment.

Although the attractive red part of a poinsettia is not a flower but bracts, or coloured leaves, they do have insignificant flowers in the centres of the bracts and these are a good guide to the health and quality of the plant. The flowers should be in the bud stage or with the stamens showing through. If the flowers have fallen off it is an indication that the plant has had its coloured bracts for much too long and will quickly lose its attractiveness.

In cold weather, it is most important to avoid buying African violets with leaves which are curled under at the edges, as this is a sign that the plant has been exposed to damaging cold conditions. Also avoid plants with wet, decaying flowers, as these will drop into the central rosette of leaves and encourage further rot.

When choosing cyclamen, look for a well-flowered plant but avoid plants with flowers which have brown edges on the petals; this indicates that flowering is nearly over. However, if an otherwise healthy plant has one or two such flowers amongst plenty of flower buds it is still worth buying because older flowers die naturally as the newer ones are formed. Once a flower has died, remove it, together with its stalk, to keep

The amount of light available is perhaps the most important factor in siting a plant indoors; this shrimp plant needs plenty of light, but some shade during the hot summer months.

the plant looking attractive and also to discourage rot. A final word of advice about cyclamen: it is not necessarily the biggest plant which is the best value. Those with considerable top growth compared to the pot size will probably have used up all the nutrients in the soil and once they are removed from the ideal growing conditions of a commercial greenhouse they often rapidly succumb to the more testing environment indoors. It is much better to select well-budded plants that are in proportion to the containers in which they are grown.

Initial siting and design

Unlike a piece of ornamental china, which is displayed entirely as a matter of personal taste, there is a certain amount of objectivity and cold science involved in siting indoor plants. A plant will show its dislike for an unsuitable position by dying, although this is usually a gradual process and reassessment at the first sign of discontent will almost certainly remedy the situation.

The amount of light available to a plant is perhaps

the most important factor; the light can be either natural sunlight or artificial light. Plants thriving in full sun should be sited as close as possible to a sunny, south or west facing window. Keep in mind, however, that light is not the only consideration. Many windows have radiators directly beneath them and the rising heat can present a real problem. Additionally, unless windows are double glazed, winter frost can penetrate the glass and physically damage tender subjects. Also solar gain during the hottest summer weather can make a window-sill much too hot for comfort. Often, the best position for a plant changes from season to season, as the plant's needs and local conditions change. Plants close to a window during winter when the amount of light is low, for example, may do best moved slightly away from the glass during the hottest and brightest summer weather. Some indoor plants, however, enjoy a brief spell outdoors during summer, in a sheltered position. Aspidistras and citrus bushes are examples. Aspidistras prefer semi-shade and full sun will ripen the wood of citrus bushes, resulting in heavier flowering the following year.

Artificial light can be used to augment a low level of natural sunlight, but this can be expensive in terms of electricity costs. Special fluorescent lights, particularly suitable for indoor plant-growing, are available and warm white tubes are also good. However, be careful not to put the artificial light source too close to the plants, as it gives off a lot of direct heat which can scorch the leaves. Some plants, such as African violet, actually do better when grown under artificial light. For such plants you can make or buy special plant-growing cases, complete with heating tubes at the bottom of the case and fluorescent lights suspended above. These cases protect plants from draughts and are economical in terms of heating. The amount of reflected light in a room can be increased by using a very pale or white paint on the walls; in this way dimly lit basement rooms can be made to seem sunnier and more attractive to both people and plants.

Direct sources of heat should be avoided, such as cookers, storage heaters, electric fires, fireplaces and even refrigerators. Draughts are equally devastating, as they increase the rate of transpiration and a plant can quickly become dessicated. For this reason, keep plants well away from air conditioning vents and badly fitted windows and doors. Draught-proof stripping fitted to windows can minimize the problem and make the room more comfortable for all concerned.

The various rooms of a house tend to have different growing conditions, each suitable for a particular type of plant. Bathrooms, for example, have a relatively high degree of humidity coupled with low levels of direct sunlight — ideal growing conditions for ferns. Kitchens may have more light but tend to have fluctuating temperatures caused by cooking, bedrooms are generally kept cooler than the sitting room and kitchen and are perfect for temperate plants, such as ivies.

Once the hazards of siting indoor plants have been identified and overcome, plants can be considered as design elements. On a functional level, plants can be used to conceal unattractive aspects of a room such as pipes or bad plasterwork. Large free-standing plants or climbers trained up trelliswork can be used as room dividers, giving privacy and a feeling of enclosure at a smaller cost than building a wall would entail.

Groups of plants can act as focal points, in much the same way as a piece of sculpture. Apart from the design aspect, plants growing together tend to benefit from the association. Watering and general maintenance will automatically become easier, and the atmosphere immediately around the plants will be relatively moist and beneficial to the plants' general health and growth. Delicate foliage can serve as a contrast to the somewhat harsh appearance of very modern furniture or humanize and soften a bare, cold-looking office space. For many people, plants give a feeling of peace and restfulness; because plants are living, they are constantly changing and developing and this process is a fascinating one to observe, over a period of weeks, months or even years. Their predictable periods of growth and flowering, followed by periods of dormancy, offer a sense of stability and contact with nature that is so often lacking in much of modern life.

Tools and equipment

For indoor growing, the most essential piece of equipment is a container. Until relatively recently, these were made of clay or earthenware. Nowadays, plastic containers have become increasingly popular and in some places it is difficult to buy a new clay pot. Both clay and plastic pots have their supporters and it is really a matter of personal preference, as it is generally accepted that plants can be equally well grown in either type. Clay pots are porous and let air and moisture through in both directions. This allows the soil inside the pot to breathe but also allows the water inside the pot to evaporate very quickly. The clay itself absorbs a great deal of water and for this reason plants grown in clay pots will need heavier

Groups of plants, attractively displayed, can act as focal points in much the same way as a piece of sculpture; here philodendron and two varieties of tradescantia are combined.

and more frequent watering than those in plastic pots.

Clay pots are heavier and relatively bulky compared to plastic ones; commercial growers, because they deal in great numbers of pots, tend to choose plastic. In addition, clay pots are more expensive, more easily broken and the labour costs involved in cleaning and sterilizing them for re-use prohibitive. Commercial considerations, however, are not necessarily relevant to home growers. Many people feel that the more natural, organic appearance of clay pots complement the foliage and flowers of a plant and do not mind the extra watering.

Clay pots should be thoroughly soaked, preferably overnight, before using to wash away any salts left from firing and also to keep the clay from absorbing excessive amounts of water from the compost. Because plastic pots are non-porous, the soil inside them tends to heat up and they should never be sited in direct sunlight for this reason.

Both clay and plastic pots are available in a variety of sizes, all measured according to the diameter at the rim. In former times, 2.5cm (1in) pots were available but these are really too small to be practical for most indoor needs, and 6.2cm (2in) is the smallest useful pot generally available. Sizes range up to 25cm (10in) and 30cm (12in) pots. Half-pots are shallow pots, half the depth of normal pots with the same diameter. These are particularly useful for shallow-rooted plants such as alpines. For visual and horticultural reasons, plants should never be put in excessively large pots. Besides looking out-of-balance, the areas of soil which are not in contact with the plant's roots may turn sour and some plants actually flower better if they are in containers slightly too small for their root ball.

The holes in the bottom of clay and plastic pots allow excess water to drain away and are essential for the well-being of the plant. Ornamental glazed pottery, bamboo or reed outer pots can be used to conceal the plastic or clay pot. Besides their attractive appearance, these cache-pots can also be functional; by filling the space between the inner and outer pot with moist peat or moss, a humid atmosphere can be created immediately around the plant.

There are a few basic tools which make indoor growing easier although they are not strictly necessary. Foremost among these is a long-spouted watering can. Unlike outdoor gardening, where water going astray does little harm, expensive carpeting and wallpaper can be damaged by unnecessary drenching, and a long-spouted watering can allows for a

Climbing plants with aerial roots, such as this philodendron, look best when given some form of substantial support.

measure of control. A sharp knife and secateurs make cutting and pruning easier and a spray gun is useful to clean and mist leaves. Those plants with hairy or furry leaves should not be exposed to water and can be cleaned with a soft-bristled brush, cotton wool, or a soft cloth. Bamboo canes are useful for supporting climbing plants together with twine or special metal rings for attaching the plant to the pole.

Many plants, particularly those with aerial roots, such as *Monstera deliciosa*, grow best when given a vertical, mossy support on which to cling. These supports can be quite expensive to buy but they are not at all difficult to make as long as you can obtain the right materials. Basically, the support has to be strong enough to bear the weight of the plant and, at the same time, not look overbearing or unsightly. It also has to be strong enough to last the life of the plant as the aerial roots take a very firm hold and the moss and stake virtually become part of the plant. Wooden supports are not advisable as they tend to rot at the base part-way through the plant's life, causing all sorts of problems. Lightweight, rigid plastic tubing is a better material, provided it can be entirely concealed by the sphagnum moss.

When measuring for the support, allow for at least 60cm (2ft) more than the height of the plant. If necessary, you can extend the height of the tubing support by inserting an additional tube, with a smaller diameter, into the top of the first one. You will need good quality sphagnum moss, not too thin in consistency. Clear nylon fishing line is ideal for binding the moss to the support, as it is very strong and does not rot. When fixing the moss to the support, remember to leave the bottom of the support free of moss, so it can be inserted into the soil. Spray the moss regularly, to keep it moist and encourage the plant's roots to cling to the support.

Watering

Watering is potentially the most lethal routine in plant maintenance and the one most likely to go wrong for the enthusiastic beginner. Giving just a drop more water is the normal response whenever a plant looks unhappy and if a plant looks in the prime of health it is often tempting to 'reward' it with an extra drink. Such thinking can be, and all too often is, fatal.

As a general rule, there are four major periods when plants need more water — in the growing season; in warm conditions; in a dry atmosphere and when in bud and flower. Many plants, however, begin their annual growth below the surface of the compost; once the roots have begun growing, leaf-growth above ground will become evident. Ideally, you should commence more frequent watering when

the roots begin to grow, but unfortunately, there is nothing visible at this time. Generally, by mid-spring most plants have begun new growth; alternatively, you can very gently tap the root ball out of the pot and look for the presence of white roots, which are young ones. Towards the end of summer, watering should gradually be decreased, as it is not a good idea to encourage the plant to put out new growth which will not have a chance to harden off.

It is often difficult to assess how frequently a plant needs watering. In general, if a pot is filled with roots there is less compost to retain water and the mass of roots will absorb it quickly. Newly potted plants will need less frequent watering than well established, even pot-bound specimens. Additionally, if a potting compost is based on peat, it will dry out much more quickly than one based on heavy loam, and will consequently need more frequent watering.

Unfortunately, the symptoms displayed for insufficient water are similar to those for excessive water. Plants which are literally drowning will have yellowed leaves which wilt and eventually fall and will most probably drop the flower buds before they open. Unfortunately, plants which are dying of thirst react the same way, and a certain amount of common sense is called for.

There are tell-tale signs about the moisture content of the soil. Clay pots, when tapped, will produce a ringing, high sound if the soil is dry and a dull thudding sound if the soil is moist. Be careful, however, as pots which are cracked will make a dull thudding sound regardless of the soil's moisture content. It is more difficult to tell with plastic pots or those containing a peat-based compost. The weight of the pot, plant and compost, when lifted, is the best indication; it will feel very light if the compost is dry. You can, after a little experience, judge fairly accurately the moisture content of the compost by pressing down on the surface with your thumb and finger; alternatively, you can purchase a soil moisture indicator.

If, after a reasonable assessment, you decide a plant needs water, then go about it in the proper way. Giving small amounts of water which slightly moisten the surface of the compost but do little else is pointless. Thorough waterings, with periods between to allow the soil to dry out slightly, are best. If the compost is so dry that it has shrunk from the sides of the pot, submerge the pot in a basin or bucket of water and leave it until air bubbles have stopped

If the compost has dried out, submerge the pot in a bucket of water until air bubbles disappear (1). Cyclamen can be watered from below to avoid wetting the corm (2). An outer container filled with moist peat creates a damp atmosphere (3).

24

rising from the surface of the water. If the compost is not bone-dry, however, do not give so much water that a heavy amount collects in the plate or saucer in which the pot is standing, as many of the nutrients contained in the compost will be washed out with the water. In any case, plants should never be left standing in dishes of water (unless they are waterside plants), as root rot will quickly set in. Peat-based composts will need more frequent checking than loam-based ones, as they tend to dry out much more quickly and, once dry, are hard to saturate thoroughly. As a rule, watering should be done in the morning. This is because the temperature is rising and the plant's need for water is greater. Also, plants left too damp over night are very vulnerable to fungal infections.

Some plants quite definitely resent water on their leaves and flowers: gloxinias and African violets, with their woolly, velvety leaves are two prime examples. Water collecting on the top of the cyclamen corm will cause rot to set in and some people advocate watering it from below. A traditional method of watering cyclamens is to place the pot on a small block of wood, 2.5cm (1in) thick in a water-tight bowl. Pour enough water in the bowl to come 2.5cm (1in) above the bottom of the flowerpot. The water will be absorbed by the roots of the cyclamen, while the corm remains dry. For African violets and gloxinias, a long-necked watering can will give some measure of control and you should be able to avoid getting water on the leaves.

For plants which enjoy a humid atmosphere, it is impractical to turn the whole of your living room into a steaming tropical jungle. Microclimates of moist atmosphere can be created by plunging the pot in question into a larger container which is packed with moist peat. Alternatively, stand the pot, or group of pots, in a large trough or tray filled with moist pebbles or gravel; the water will gently evaporate into the air immediately surrounding the plant.

Feeding
As with watering, feeding is largely a matter of striking a happy medium between starving a plant of nutrients and gorging it. Enthusiastic generosity in the matter of feeding is no substitute for common sense combined with a knowledge of the right time to feed. As a general rule, dormant plants should not be given fertilizers, nor should cuttings or

If you are unable to water a plant while on holiday, there are several ways to meet its water needs for short periods of time: strips of absorbent cloth with one end tucked firmly in the soil and the other in a pan of water (1), an air-tight, transparent plastic bag (2) or water diffuser (3).

seedlings without fully formed roots. Plants which have been left to dry out inadvertantly should be given plenty of water to revive them before any fertilizers are given, as dessicated plants can be harmed by taking up nutrients.

Nutrients are needed during a plant's growing season, particularly when it is about to flower and when it is in flower. Tell-tale signs of growth are the appearance of young shoots and leaves. Should an immature plant fail to grow in the normal growing season, or should it produce unnaturally yellow leaves, this may be due to a lack of food. Be careful, however, as yellow leaves can also be symptomatic of insufficient or excessive water, or too little or too much light and it is really a process of elimination to discover the cause.

There are basically two types of plant food: organic and inorganic. The former are those chemical compounds containing carbon and are usually derived from living organisms. Manure, spent hops, garden compost and seaweed are bulky organic manures, while dried blood, hoof and horn and bone meal are non-bulky organic fertilizers. Inorganic fertilizers are those not containing carbon; artificially manufactured, the nutrients are immediately available to the plant. Basic slag, sulphate of potash and sulphate of ammonia are examples.

Whether a fertilizer is organic or inorganic, plants can only absorb the nutrients contained in them in liquid form. Bulky organic manures generally take longer for the nutrients to break down to a form readily available to plants, and this process of decomposing is aided by the various micro-organisms found in soil. While eminently suitable for outdoor gardening, where their bulky substance will do much to improve the texture of the soil, there are certain drawbacks to using organic manures indoors. Besides the odour, they often harbour pests, diseases and weed seeds and they are not really suitable for the small-scale activity of growing potted indoor plants.

Inorganic fertilizers are much more practical for indoor growing. Although they do little to improve the texture of the compost, proprietary potting composts, whether soil-based or peat-based, are already of the right consistency and do not need the bulk provided by organic manures. Many are available in concentrated liquid form and must be diluted before use. Always follow manufacturer's instructions, as excessive amounts of nutrients can be very damaging to the plant. They are also available as soluble powder and pellets, and again, manufacturer's instructions must be strictly followed. Inorganic fertilizers contain the proper amounts of

Platycerium bifurcatum, or stag's horn fern, is epiphytic; using tree branches for support it feeds from nutrients dissolved in rainwater in its cup-shaped frond base.

the three basic elements necessary for a plant to survive: nitrates for growth and rich green leaf colour, potash for the encouragement of flowers and fruit, as well as for keeping the growth from becoming too lush and soft, and phosphates for a healthy stem and root system. As peat-based composts have virtually no inherent fertilizers, plants growing in this medium will need more frequent feeding than those grown in soil-based, John Innes compounds, which already contain a certain amount of slow-acting nutrients. Besides watering nutrients into the soil, they can also be sprayed directly onto the leaves; such foliar sprays are often used as quick stimulants for ailing plants.

Repotting

Potting up, potting on and repotting are all similar processes. However, they all occur at different stages of a plant's development. First comes potting up. This is the initial transfer of newly rooted seedlings or cuttings from the seed or cutting compost, which has no nutritional value, into individual pots containing slightly richer compost. Seedlings tend to come up quite thickly in the seed pan and cuttings are usually placed close together until they root. Once germination and rooting have occurred, the young plants need less crowded conditions so by potting them up individually, each plant has a chance to develop a good root system.

When the seedlings are large enough to handle or the cuttings are well-rooted, begin potting them up. A useful tool to have for this operation is a pair of long and finely tipped tweezers. Normally the tweezers are held in the left hand so that their prongs, gently grip the stem of the seedling beneath the bottom set of leaves. During the lifting and transferring, hold the seedling in place very gently by one of the leaves. Before placing the young plant into its new pot, make a depression in the compost large enought to accommodate the roots. Use your index finger or the end of a pencil to make the depression. You need then only gently cover the roots with potting compost pushed in from around each depression, using the fingers or the flat end of a tongue depressor. Make sure the roots of the seedlings are covered and that they are planted deep enough. The initial pot into which the seedling or rooted cutting is placed should be quite small, 7.5cm (3in) is by far large enough; if the pots are too big the soil will turn sour and no advantage will be gained by the plant. For several days after potting up, shade the plants from direct sunlight until they resume growth and make sure they are well watered.

Potting on is the next stage and is normally carried out when a plant has outgrown its container. There

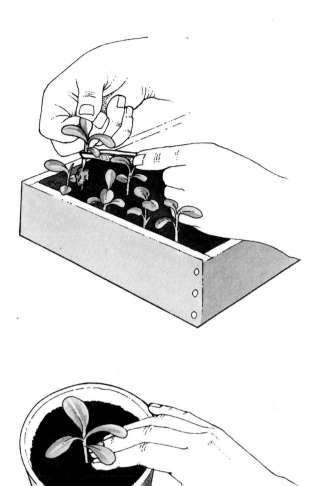

Once seedlings have germinated in a seed box or pan, the resulting seedlings tend to be overcrowded and can quickly become drawn and spindly from too much competition. As soon as they are large enough to handle, pot them up individually into small pots, firming the compost with your fingers.

are several signs which indicate that an immature plant is ready for potting on; it may have stopped growing, or roots may be appearing out of the bottom of the drainage hole at the base of the container. The secret of success with potting on is to increase the size of the pot only slightly each time; as a general rule, there should be no more than 2.5cm (1in) of space between the root ball of the plant and the sides of the new pot. This empty space is filled with fresh compost into which the roots will quickly grow. Most potting on is done in late winter or early spring, while the plant is still dormant, to avoid shocking the plant.

Roots growing out of the drainage hole are a good indication that the plant has become pot-bound and needs potting on (1). Using a slightly larger pot which is scrupulously clean and contains fresh compost, transplant gently and carefully (2). Potting on completed: note the space left at the top of the pot for water and the bottom layer of drainage material (3).

Make sure the pots into which the plants are transferred are scrupulously clean. If there are particles of soil clinging to the side, roots will become entangled in them and when the time comes to repot the plant, it will be practically impossible to remove the plant without damaging the roots.

Put a layer of drainage material at the bottom of the pot. It is essential that the plant will be at the same level in its new pot as it was in its previous one and, if need be, put a layer of fresh compost above the drainage material to bring the level up. Whenever potting, use moist but not too wet compost. If it is saturated and dripping water it will be difficult to compact properly and may congeal into a solid, airless mass of soil.

Holding your fingers round the base of the stem with the palm of your hand covering the soil, invert the pot and give it a sharp tap on the base. The plant, with its root ball intact, should slip easily from the pot. If it does not, after several repeated attempts, you may have to sacrifice the container. Carefully slit the side of plastic pots with a sharp secateur and remove the plant. If the pot is clay, then gently crack it with a hammer; be careful, however, as excessive enthusiasm when cracking open clay pots may lead to damage to the root ball.

Once the plant is free of its container, inspect the bottom of the root ball and carefully remove any pieces of crocks which may have become entangled in the roots. Then lower the plant into its new pot and, holding it with one hand, carefully work the new soil round the roots with the other. After the sides have been filled, give the pot a sharp rap on a table surface to help the plant and compost to settle. If the compost is peat based, compress it down with your fingers as well; alternatively, use a wood soil dibber with a rounded bottom. Make sure the final level of the soil is about 2.5cm (1in) below the rim of the pot, to allow for ease of watering. As with potting up, the plants should receive shelter from strong sunlight and slightly more water than normal until they have recovered from potting on.

Repotting refers to the process of transferring a mature plant which has completely filled its container with roots into another pot of the same size. This is usually done while the plant is dormant. The advantage gained from such a manoeuvre is that old, worn-out compost is replaced with fresh compost. It sometimes involves reducing the size of the rootball to encourage the production of fresh roots. Bonsai plants are regularly repotted to keep them healthy, but it is not a process to be embarked on lightly. If a plant has reached full size and appears not to thrive, it may be due to lack of nutrients, which can be remedied by giving a dilute liquid feed

or a top dressing of fresh compost. Alternatively, try changing its position in relation to the amount of light or warmth it receives; leave repotting as a last resort.

A healthy and well-maintained group planting: the vertical dieffenbachia is set off by the trailing stems of the delicate Ficus pumila and the golden variegated Scindapsus aureus.

General maintenance

Besides watering, feeding and potting on, there are numerous small tasks which, if conscientiously carried out, make all the difference between a meagre plant and a flourishing one. Little and often might be the best guide; do not treat your plants like cupboards, to be spring-cleaned once a year and ignored for the next twelve months. If you see a dead or diseased leaf, remove it immediately. Besides improving the general appearance of the plant, it will discourage the various pests and diseases which thrive on dead plant tissue. The same goes for yellow leaves; once a leaf which is normally green turns yellow it will not recover and should be removed and consigned to the dustbin. Do not confuse yellowed leaves with the slight lack of colouring which occurs when plants are in need of feeding; the leaves which are removed should be bright yellow or else withered and lifeless.

Climbing plants that produce untidy growth should have their stems tied (not too tightly) to a suitable support. Some climbing plants, such as ivy, tend to lose most of their lower leaves and produce young growth only at the top of the stems; these will be vastly improved in appearance if some of the longer growth is trained downwards to fill in the gaps at the base.

Plants with large, naturally glossy leaves should be dusted now and again to keep the leaves shiny. Although all sorts of chemical concoctions can be purchased to spray on the leaves for a glossy appearance, they can be positively harmful to some plants and should never be used on the soft young growth

Vigorous climbing plants such as bougainvillea can get out of hand if growth is not controlled. Stems can be trained up bamboo or plastic poles or in a circle around wire.

at the top of a plant. A quick wipe with a soft duster will suffice most of the time. Occasionally use a moistened soft cloth or sponge to do a thorough job.

To counteract the effects of a dry atmosphere, periodically spray the leaves of plants with tepid water. Not all plants appreciate a humid atmosphere, however; saintpaulias and other downy-leaved plants should not be sprayed. As a rule, plants exposed to full sunlight should not be sprayed as the droplets of water on the leaves can cause scorch.

Perhaps the most controversial of all aspects of plant care, is that of plant psychology. Although the commercial grower of indoor plants may be a trifle cynical about the idea of plants as responsive, sensitive creatures, when he is surrounded by literally millions of them during the course of his working life, the householder can, and frequently does, adopt an entirely different attitude. For many people, plants grown indoors take on a completely different meaning from those in the vegetable garden and even decorative outdoor plants. They are often looked upon as friends and it is not unusual to find a favourite monstera named Fred, or a rubber plant named George, and so on. Plants received as gifts are sometimes named after the donor, thus forming a living link between the two people involved and should anything unfortunate happen to the plant, the feelings of guilt become even stronger because of what the plant symbolized.

Talking and even singing to plants in order to get positive responses from them, by way of bigger and better leaves and flowers, has long been practised. This seems to get results in two ways. Obviously, if one stops to have a word with the Swiss cheese plant when passing, one is more likely to notice any defects, such as excessive dryness at the roots or the presence of pests.

Secondly, recent experiments have shown that plants actually do respond positively to such human pleasures as the presence of classical music. Likewise, electrodes from lie-detectors attached to plants and used to measure their responses to various situations have indicated that plants do experience rudimentary pain and fear when harmed or threatened with harm. These same tests, which were carried out by an American lie detector expert, indicated that plants have the ability to remember specific incidents and would react negatively when someone who had previously harmed them reappeared.

Although these conclusions do not automatically commit one to thinking of plants as quasi-human, they do widen the scope of interaction between plants and people. They also suggest the possibility that the proverbial green fingers is not so much a matter of luck as empathy to which plants happily respond.

Propagation

When raising new plants from seed, cuttings, division or air layering, a few simple rules will ensure a high rate of success. Perhaps the most important is cleanliness. Everything associated with the operation must be spotlessly clean; previously used pots and boxes must be thoroughly scrubbed and the propagation mixture must be sterile (not a handful of soil from the garden).

To produce roots of their own, all cuttings of indoor plants will require a minimum temperature

Impatiens, or busy lizzy, benefits from periodical pinching out of growing tips to keep the plant from getting leggy.

of around 18°C (65°F); slightly higher temperatures are, on the whole, beneficial, but very hot and dry conditions can be calamitous. There are many small propagating cases available at a reasonable cost and these are ideal for small cuttings. More expensive propagating cases are available, with a built-in heating element, but there is no need to go to the extra expense if the propagator can be placed over

31

Busy lizzies are among the easiest plants to propagate, simply place cuttings in a bottle of water to root.

Spider plants produce large quantities of plantlets which can be potted up individually and detached from the mother.

a radiator that is operating constantly, day and night. Keeping an even, steady temperature is important, as few cuttings will do well in fluctuating temperatures.

Given proper cleanliness and temperature, the most important factor is the propagating material itself. Scrappy odds and ends taken from tired and sickly plants will almost inevitably fail. Select firm and healthy material for propagation or the whole exercise will be a waste of time.

Perhaps the best standard cutting compost is one composed of equal parts, by volume, of fresh peat and sharp sand. The sand must be sharp and the peat sphagnum and not sedge, as the latter holds too much water and is less free draining; Vermiculite is another good cutting compost. Whatever the compost, it should be moist enough for a little water to show between your fingers when a handful is compressed.

All this having been said, there is many a healthy houseplant which started life on its own in nothing more than a bottle filled with water with a piece of kitchen foil pressed over the top — the stem of the cutting is pushed through a hole in the middle of the foil so the stem reaches water and the leaf rests on the foil. Warmth and light are still necessary, but indirect light is best; any cutting exposed to full sunlight will simply shrivel up. Some good plants to propagate by this elementary bottle of water and foil method are African violets, ivies, busy lizzies and spider plants. Success is almost inevitable with these plants and, having been encouraged, more difficult subjects may then be attempted.

Plants which produce tiny, complete plantlets on the ends of runners, or stolons, are the easiest of all to propagate. Besides the spider plant (*Chlorophytum comosum*), mother-of-thousands (*Saxifraga sarmentosa*) is another good subject. Pegged down in any reasonable growing mixture, these young plantlets will quickly produce roots of their own while still attached by the stolon to the parent plant. Once well-rooted, they can be severed from the parent plant and potted up to grow on independently. Unlike most other cuttings, a peat and sand mixture is not usually suitable, as the young plants quickly become starved of nourishment and lose their colour.

Another simple yet successful method of propagation is the division of a large plant, complete with roots, into several new individuals. Aspidistras are suitable subjects for division, but there are many others. Before beginning, water the plant thoroughly; once moist, remove the plant and carefully shake off as much of the potting mixture as possible. Then gently tease apart the roots to provide several independent plants. Older clumps, however, will require more than teasing apart; it may be necessary to use a knife to divide the tough rhizomes, or even a sharp spade. Whatever the method of division, the new plants should be potted up as soon as possible into a rich growing mixture. Peat and sand is inadvisable, as these plants already have functioning roots and will need a growing medium which can provide nutrients.

Its long, arching stolons bearing perfectly formed plants at the tips make chlorophytum an attractive subject.

Aspidistras, or cast iron plants, can be propagated by division in spring; carefully prise apart the roots.

To keep new cuttings from wilting until roots have formed, enclose them in an air-tight, transparent polythene bag.

Cuttings are slightly more difficult because when they are removed from the parent plant they continue to lose water through the leaves, or transpire and, as they have no roots with which moisture can be replaced, they will quickly die. Most commercial growers, and many keen amateurs, have overcome this problem with a piece of equipment called a mist unit. This apparatus contains a series of fine jets of water which are activated either according to a set time clock or by an electronic 'leaf' which measures the amount of moisture over the bed of cuttings. The mist unit ensures that the surfaces of the cuttings never dry out and a greater success rate ensues.

Mist units are expensive, however, and there are other methods of overcoming this problem which are suitable for the amateur dealing with a small number of plants. Many of the easier plants, such as ivies, do perfectly well if the cuttings are put in small pots which are then covered with a thin sheet of polythene. The polythene will considerably reduce transpiration and the cuttings should root within two or three weeks. Remove the polythene periodically to reduce the risk of rot setting in; as soon as the cuttings show signs of growth the polythene should be removed completely. Alternatively, cuttings placed in small pots can be protected by enclosing them in airtight polythene bags which are supported by one or two canes to prevent the bags from collapsing onto the cuttings.

The advent of hormone rooting powders and liquids has made propagation very much easier and the success rate higher. With hormone liquids, the cutting is removed from the parent plant and dipped in the liquid rooting stimulant before being inserted in the rooting medium. With powder, cuttings should be dipped in water first, so the powder will adhere more readily.

It is a good idea to make a hole in the rooting compost to the depth that the cutting is likely to reach. It should not be too deep, as the end of the cutting should rest on the rooting mixture at the bottom of the hole. If the hole is too deep, the cuttings will swing in mid-air and be unable to root satisfactorily. Once the cuttings are in position, give a final watering, using a fine rose, before covering the cuttings with polythene or the lid of the propagating case.

Although much is written about the best time of the year to take cuttings, the vast majority of foliage plant cuttings will root at almost any time of year, given proper heat and moisture. In less than perfect conditions, however, late spring and early summer are best. The plant, once it has rooted, then has a whole growing season before it and its chances of survival are quite high.

Ficus robusta, the rubber plant, is one of the most popular indoor plants and has a definite time of year when cuttings should be taken. In the winter months the plant is dormant and less sap is likely to be lost in the process of taking cuttings. The top section of the plant, with three leaves attached, will produce a very respectable-looking plant in a relatively short time, while cuttings taken with a single leaf and piece of stem from lower down the plant will be rather sparse and awkward looking for quite some time. To take the cuttings, use a sharp knife or secateurs and allow the wet end of the cuttings to dry before inserting into a peat and sand mixture. A minimum temperature of 21°C (70°F) is needed and roots should be produced in about a month. New leaves should appear about two weeks after the roots; although quite small at first, they will quickly increase in size provided that the cuttings are not left too long in the mixture of peat and sand.

Over-grown rubber plants, which are too tall and spindly to be attractive, can be used to make two plants of more manageable size by the process of air layering. In this method of propagation, the top half of the plant is encouraged to produce roots of its own before it is actually severed from the main stem. Decide where you want the roots to form and then remove the closest leaf. Make a notch in the

Scindapsus aureus, or golden pothos, often needs pruning to keep it from growing leggy. Use the cuttings taken in spring or summer to form new plants.

35

To air layer a rubber plant, nick the stem and keep it open by inserting a pebble (1). Dust with rooting powder and wrap *sphagnum moss around the area (2). Secure moss with clear polythene (3). Detach and pot up when roots have formed (4).*

stem about 5cm (2in) in length and half the thickness of the stem. Hold the cut open by inserting a small pebble between the two sections of stem and dust the wound with rooting powder. Then wrap moist sphagnum moss around the entire area, securing it with clear polythene and soft twine. Signs of roots should be visible in about two months; when an ample number of them can be seen, remove the polythene and leave the moss ball intact. Cut the newly rooted plant from the mother plant just below the roots and insert it in a rich growing medium; maintain the temperature at 21°C (70°F) and keep the compost on the dry side until the plant has become established.

The parent plant will produce several new shoots from just below the cut and a bushier, well-furnished specimen should result. Unfortunately, the Swiss cheese plant (*Monstera deliciosa*), does not respond to air layering, and tends to remain ungainly looking when the top growth is removed. These plants are not easily propagated from cuttings, and almost all commercially grown plants are raised from seed sown in a high temperature.

Another form of layering involves placing plants with long strands of growth, such as *Ficus pumila*, near a boxful of potting mixture and directing the strands into the mixture, where they will root naturally. Once strong-growing roots have formed, the new plants can be severed from the parent and potted up.

Although African violet cuttings will root quite happily in water, a higher success rate will be achieved if the cuttings are inserted in a sand and peat mixture and kept at a constant temperature of 21°C (70°F). Select leaves which are firm, green and free from blemish and insert them gently into the rooting medium. Because the leaves are soft and furry, a very humid atmosphere may encourage leaf-rot; do not cover the cuttings with polythene or wet the leaves while watering the rooting medium. Each leaf will eventually produce a cluster of small plants around the base of its stalk and these can be detached and potted up, either teased apart and planted individually, or all in one pot. Although the plants may look bigger and better initially if planted in one pot, this practice usually results in less attractive mature plants, with flowers and leaves growing in all directions. Additionally, young plants should not be allowed to flower prematurely and as a rule the first flower buds should be removed as soon as they are seen.

Poinsettia cuttings are taken from new growth in early summer; 10cm (4in) sections are taken, cutting just below a leaf. Remove the bottom leaf and insert the cuttings as quickly as possible into pure peat. Despite the speed of the operation, they will still wilt alarmingly and will need frequent and regular spraying if they are to survive. Once they have made a reasonable amount of root the plants can be potted up into a rich mixture; when they have settled down, remove the growing tips to produce a bushier, more attractive plant.

To propagate African violets, select and detach strong, healthy leaves from the plant.

Gently insert these into a rooting medium kept at a temperature of 21°C (70°F).

Once roots have formed, small leaves will appear at the base. Well-grown African violets (above).

Sansevieria cuttings are slightly out-of-the-ordinary in that they are made from cutting the main stem into sections and pressing them, vertically, into boxes filled with pure peat. Once roots and leaves have formed, the original stem section is buried when the new plant is potted up.

Raising new plants from seed may seem less exciting than other methods of propagation, but it is certainly the most economical way of aquiring the greatest number of plants in the shortest possible time. Do not skimp on the cost of a packet of seed or the entire exercise may prove disappointing.

Use boxes or shallow pans filled with a peat and sand mixture; press down the compost gently — never ram it. Finally, moisten the surface with water from a watering can fitted with a fine rose and sow the seed.

Follow directions on the seed packet for the best results; after sowing, cover the box or pan with a plate of glass and then a sheet of newspaper. Lift and turn the glass regularly and once germination has occurred, remove the newspaper so the seedlings are exposed to light. Leave the seedlings to grow on until they are large enough to handle, then lift them by their leaves and transfer them, properly spaced out, into similar boxes or pots filled with a conventional potting mixture.

Given reasonable amounts of warmth, moisture and light, a very wide range of plants can be grown from seed, including such exotics as coffee and banana plants. Although it may take some time from sowing to the fully grown specimen and plenty of patience is required, many people find this method of plant propagation the most rewarding.

Propagation of ferns from spores is a similar operation to propagation of new plants from seeds. Fill a shallow clay pan with a mixture of equal parts (by volume) of peat and loam, with a little sharp sand added for drainage and a little charcoal to keep the

After sowing seeds, cover the pan with a sheet of glass and newspaper to keep the atmosphere moist and dark until germination has occurred (1). Then remove the paper to expose the young plants to sunlight; removing the glass gives them room to grow and reduces their vulnerability to damping off (2). Cuttings which have not yet rooted are liable to wilt and may need frequent and regular spraying to keep the leaves turgid. Poinsettia cuttings are a case in point (3). Sansevieria can be easily propagated from leaf cuttings inserted vertically in a sandy compost; tiny complete plants will grow from the newly-formed roots (4).
Opposite: a well-grown nephrolepis. Propagation is by division, by pegging down its creeping stems and severing the new young plant when rooted, or from spores collected from the undersides of the leaves.

38

compost sweet. To collect the spores, take a frond which has dark brown spore cases on its under side and put it in a paper bag. Shake the bag vigorously to release the spores, which will then collect at the bottom of the bag. Before sowing, firm the surface of the compost and moisten with water from a fine-rosed watering can. Once the spores have been sown, cover the pan with a plate of glass and put the pan in a larger container which has been partially filled with water. It is essential that the compost is never allowed to dry out; the pan should be of clay to allow the water to permeate. It should also be kept out of direct sunlight, but constant warmth must be maintained. From one to three months later, depending on the type of fern propagated, a

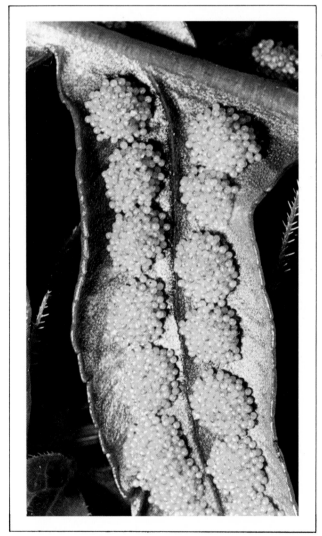

Underside of the hardy common fern, Polypodium vulgare, showing the clusters of ripe spores ready for dispersal.

moss-like growth will appear on the surface of the compost; this is the prothallus, an intermediary stage which will in turn produce tiny new ferns.

Once these ferns appear, remove the glass so they get plenty of fresh air. When they are large enough to handle, prick out groups of tiny ferns into pots filled with similar compost and put them in a shaded, airy place. When they have grown slightly larger, pot them up into individual containers.

Dealing with pests and diseases

The warm, moist growing conditions that make for first-class, healthy indoor plants are, unfortunately, perfect for innumerable pests and diseases which also thrive in warm moist environments. By far the best step in controlling such problems is a preventative one, that is, to avoid introducing them into the house. Although this may appear as an over-simplification, many a newly-bought plant has arrived home with the added bonus of greenfly, whitefly or mealybug. Before buying a plant, inspect it thoroughly for any signs of infection or infestation.

The most common problems you are likely to encounter are listed below, together with method of control. No matter what sort of pesticide or fungicide you use, keep in mind that results can be disastrous for the plant in question and also dangerous to the user, if instructions are not followed exactly. Always wear rubber gloves when handling pesticides. Plants should be taken into the protected area of a garage or shed where fumes will not blow about and the plant should not be exposed to strong sunlight immediately after spraying the foliage. It is also a good idea to leave the plant out of the house until all the unpleasant odours connected with spraying have disappeared. Often, a single application will not be sufficient and repeat applications should be made according to the manufacturer's instructions. When spraying, pay particular attention to the undersides of the leaves, where pests would otherwise be sheltered from the spray. Red spider mites and scale insects are notorious for preferring leaf undersides.

Aphids
These are also known as greenfly and blackfly depending on the colour of the species. They are small, plump and usually wingless pests, and are always found in large colonies. One or other species of aphids attack almost every cutltivated plant. Most species are foliage feeders but some attack the woody parts and others feed on the roots. When feeding they force their needle-like mouthparts into the plant sap stream and pump in digestive juices before sucking up the sap. The saliva is often toxic to the plant tissue and can cause severe discolouration of the leaves. The removal of the sap weakens the plant and the punctures can act as a point of entry for

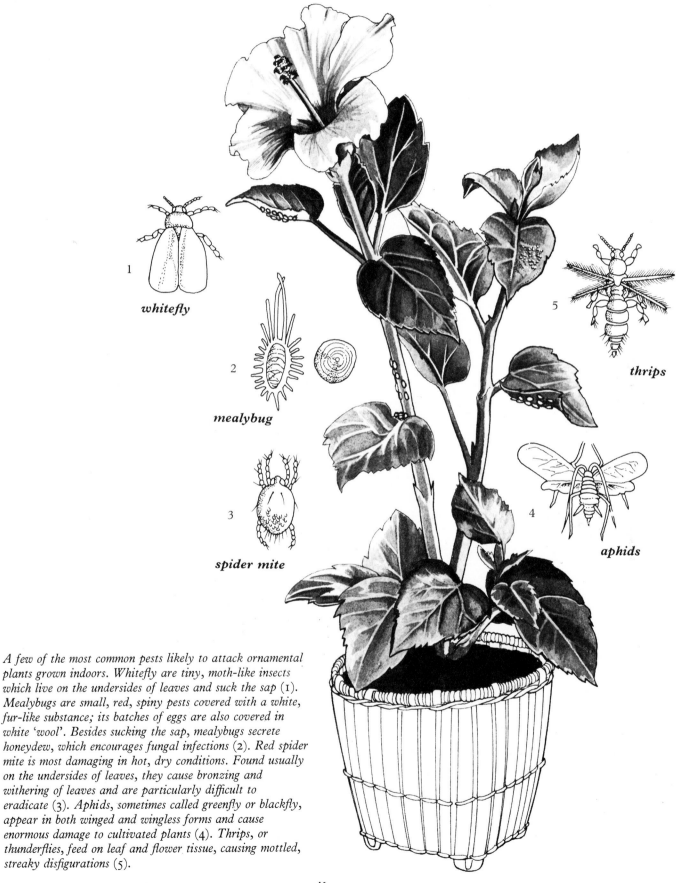

1
whitefly

2
mealybug

3
spider mite

5
thrips

4
aphids

A few of the most common pests likely to attack ornamental plants grown indoors. Whitefly are tiny, moth-like insects which live on the undersides of leaves and suck the sap (1). Mealybugs are small, red, spiny pests covered with a white, fur-like substance; its batches of eggs are also covered in white 'wool'. Besides sucking the sap, mealybugs secrete honeydew, which encourages fungal infections (2). Red spider mite is most damaging in hot, dry conditions. Found usually on the undersides of leaves, they cause bronzing and withering of leaves and are particularly difficult to eradicate (3). Aphids, sometimes called greenfly or blackfly, appear in both winged and wingless forms and cause enormous damage to cultivated plants (4). Thrips, or thunderflies, feed on leaf and flower tissue, causing mottled, streaky disfigurations (5).

41

fungal and bacterial diseases. Aphids are also major carriers of viral diseases. Finally, aphids disfigure plants by covering the surfaces with sticky honeydew which often becomes infected with sooty moulds.

The major problem with aphids is their enormous breeding rate. Fortunately, this is reduced by natural predators such as ladybird and lacewing, but even so, damaging infestations can build up very quickly. This emphasizes the need to watch for any sign of trouble.

Root aphids, which can be very damaging to cacti, succulents and many ornamental plants, are moved from one plant to another by ants which 'farm' them for their honeydew. Another specialized species is the woolly aphid which is covered with white waxy wool and feeds on branches and pruning cuts, causing unsightly gall-like growths.

Foliage-feeding aphids are easy to control, being susceptible to many systemic and non-systemic insecticides.

The control of woolly aphids presents rather more of a problem because of the protective waxy covering and it is therefore necessary to use a forceful spray of malathion, gamma-HCH or dimethoate.

Root aphids are the most difficult to deal with. Either lift the plants and then wash the roots free of aphids or apply soil drenches of malathion or pirimiphos-methyl.

Mealybugs

These pests look rather like woolly aphids because of their covering of powdery white wax. They are sap suckers, attacking the stems and leaves, and will generally be found around the buds and leaf joints. Some species feed on roots and are particulary common on cacti and succulents. Mealybugs are resistant to many pesticides although malathion and dimethoate are still effective. An added complication in controlling mealybugs is that cacti and succulents tend to be senstive to many chemical sprays. Tests should therefore be made on single plants or on a few leaves of each species to ensure that the spray has no adverse effects on the plant. Wiping the leaves with methylated spirits is another form of control, if rather cumbersome.

Whitefly

Adult whitefly are rather like tiny white moths with a covering of powdery wax on their bodies. They are usually found feeding on the undersides of the younger leaves and flutter about if disturbed. The females lay eggs on the undersides of the host plant's leaves. These hatch out into small, flattened oval green scale-like larvae which feed by sucking the plant sap. Eventually they turn into waxy pupae from

which the new adults later emerge, the whole cycle taking 3-4 weeks.

The commonest species attacking ornamental plants is the greenhouse whitefly. During the summer this may also attack outdoor plants.

Until recently, whitefly were a particularly difficult to control because only the adults were susceptible to available insecticides. Consequently repeated treatments had to be given over a period of at least a month in order to deal with new generations of adults which emerged from the younger stages. Fortunately, some new insecticides, notably resmethrin, bioresmethrin and pirimiphos-methyl are active against the larval stage, though even these chemicals have no effect on the eggs and pupae. Still it is now possible to control whitefly effectively by using a programme of three sprays at 3- to 4-day intervals, directing the spray on to the undersides of the leaves where the insects are feeding. A solid bar containing insecticide can also be hung up indoors to control these pests.

Scale insects

Scale insects spend most of their lives firmly fixed to the plant surface where the adult females look rather like miniature limpets. The eggs of some species are protected by white waxy wool but in others they are simply retained within the scale of the female crawlers which move to a suitable feeding site and then settle down to suck the plant sap. They are common on many plants, indoor and outdoor, and are a particular nuisance in the greenhouse. All species produce sticky honeydew which becomes infected with sooty moulds.

Scale insects are difficult to control because both the eggs and the adults are protected by the tough scale. Spray treatments with dimethoate, malathion or pirimiphos-methyl may be used giving two or three applications at 14-day intervals. This treatment is best started when the eggs have hatched and the young crawlers are still on the move. If the infestation is not too heavy the adults can be scraped off or removed with cotton wool soaked in methylated spirits and wrapped around an orange stick.

Thrips

Thrips are minute, slender, dark-coloured insects. They feed on the underside of the leaves by scraping the surface and then sucking up the sap. Leaf damage shows up as a yellow or silvery mottling while infested flowers develop white streaks. Attacked plants become stunted and deformed. Thrips also transmit virus diseases. Both indoor and outdoor plants are subject to attack but this pest is more serious indoors where its breeding is encouraged by hot dry conditions and is continuous instead of being restricted to summer as it is outdoors. Thrips are fairly readily controlled by most insecticides. Treatment should be given at the first sign of attack and repeated at 7- to 10-day intervals as necessary.

Mites

Mites, including the well-known red spider mites, are extremely small creatures, being just visible to the naked eye as globular pinheads. They are not insects but are included as they are dealt with in a similar way. They are common and widespread sap-feeding pests, both indoors and out. Attacked foliage quickly develops a yellow speckling which later becomes bronzed. Some species produce silken webs which enable them to pass from one plant to another.

Mites are rather difficult to control as only a limited number of pesticides are effective against these pests. Malathion, dimethoate, resmethrin and biroresmethrin all give a degree of control. Even so, repeated applications at 7- to 10-day intervals are usually necessary because of the resistance of the eggs to most garden chemicals. Do not keep using the same insecticide as this will result in a quicker build-up of resistance. As mites thrive in dry, over-crowded conditions, keeping an adequately humid atmosphere around the plants will control the numbers indoors.

Botrytis

This fungal infection is a very common problem, both indoors and out. It is usually associated with cool, damp growing conditions and excessive moisture. Its common name, grey mould, is very descriptive of the main symptom: fluffy, grey growths on the leaves, stems and flowers of infected plants. Initially, the disease enters the plant through a wound or through dead or dying tissue and dead leaves or flowers left on a plant are particularly vulnerable. Because the spores of botrytis are always present in the air, poor growing conditions can quickly lead to a severe attack.

The best precaution is to ensure that plants are not overcrowded and that air can circulate freely. If a plant is slightly infected, remove and burn those parts of the plant showing symptoms. Improve the growing conditions by raising the temperature, both night and day, and giving more ventilation. Badly infected plants should be removed and destroyed, as it is unlikely they will recover.

Mildew

This is the name given to a type of plant disease which shows in the leaves, shoots and sometimes the flowers of infected plants as a surface covering of a powdery white or greyish fungus. Basically, there are two types of mildew. Powdery mildews are entirely superficial and grow on the surfaces of a plant as a white powdery coating; chains of spores are produced in the coating and these spores spread the infection.

The downy mildews grow deeply into the inner tissues and send up threads through the surface which produce infective summer spores; the spores are eventually released into the soil. Downy mildews are seen on the surface only as a greyish patch of furry growth but they are far more injurious than the superficial powdery mildews.

Plants which are grown in poorly ventilated, moist air conditions are particularly vulnerable and also plants which are too dry at the roots. At the first sign of mildew, remove and destroy the infected parts and spray the plant with a fungicide. It is equally essential to find the plant a more congenial growing position.

Before using a fungicide, make sure that it is chemically suitable for the particular plant. Proprietary sprays containing dinocap or zineb are most common, but chrysanthemums and begonias should be sprayed or dusted with a sulphur-based fungicide.

Virus

A virus is a minute particle, visible only under the electron microscope, which causes disorders or diseases in living cells. Yellow or brown spots, streak or ring patterns on the leaves may be an indication of virus. Other viral symptoms on the leaves are dark green areas along the veins, a loss of green colour in the veins or a complete yellowing of the leaf. Streaks may appear on stems of infected plants. On flowers, white flecks or streaks of an unexpected colour or distortion may indicate viral infection. Less distinct symptoms of viral infection are a general stunting and reduction of vigour.

Some viruses adhere to the mouth parts of insects feeding on infected plants and they are then carried to healthy plants. Others are absorbed into the digestive system of the insect and from there pass into the salivary glands where the virus multiplies. When feeding, the insect injects saliva containing virus particles into plants and will remain a disease carrier all its life.

Because insects are major transmitters of viral infections, the elimination of pests is the best preventive measure against the spread of viruses. Plants propagated from infected material will contain virus particles, so make sure your source of plants is reputable. Regular inspection of all plants is another good precaution; suspect plants should be destroyed, as once a plant is infected there is no known cure.

HOUSEPLANT SPECIALITIES

Although the same basic rules apply to the majority of houseplants, some 'specialities' such as bottle gardens or bonsai trees do require some distinctive treatment to succeed in the home.

Bottle gardens

When growing a large selection of indoor plants it is impossible to provide within the walls of one room conditions that will be ideal for them all; ivy, for example, prefers a cool and dry atmosphere while philodendrons like a warmer and moister environment. Similarly, many ferns require close, damp and warm conditions which are totally impossible to provide in an average room.

One way of overcoming this difficulty is to offer the more demanding plants an environment of their own, a mini-greenhouse within a room. The Victorian Wardian case was the first such indoor greenhouse and its modern counterpart is the bottle garden, although a wide variety of glass containers can be used to achieve the same effect. Very elaborate and expensive containers can be bought, made of panels of clear and stained glass and leading, but a tropical fish tank is just as effective, far less expensive and is actually much easier to plant and maintain than a conventional bottle garden. A fish tank merely needs the lid removed, while the narrow neck of bottle gardens makes access to the plants more difficult and requires an assortment of improvised tools attached to long canes to keep the plants well tended.

Whatever the container, it must be clean, both inside and out, and warm soapy water is best. The glass should be rinsed and allowed to dry thoroughly before the potting mixture is introduced to avoid compost sticking to the side of the container. If you are using a bottle or carboy, make sure the cardboard is removed from the lid; if left in, mildew or other fungus will be encouraged to grow. When the container is completely clean and dry, use a cardboard tube to put in a layer of washed gravel to provide for drainage. Follow this with a layer of charcoal lumps and finally a layer of moist and crumbly peat or potting compost. The soil can either be loam or peat-based but it must be sterilized to kill unwanted seeds and pests. In a closed environment, it is absolutely imperative that the plants themselves are healthy and pest free as these conditions form a perfect environment for most diseases.

The choice of plants for a bottle garden should be made with care. It is best to avoid flowering plants, such as African violets, as once the flowers have faded they must be removed from the container or fungal infection will quickly set in. It is not only important to use small plants at the outset, but also to know that they grow slowly. *Selaginella* is a case in point; this delicate fern-like foliage plant seems at first glance eminently suitable for the bottle garden. If given ideal surroundings, it will grow at a rapid pace and quickly smother neighboring plants. *Pilea*

is another highly invasive plant well kept out of a bottle garden with mixed planting. However, both of these plants are attractive, and might be tried used on their own in large containers.

Among the most attractive foliage plants for colour are varieties of crotons (*Codiaeum reidii* and *Codiaeum holufiana*) begonias (*Begonia rex* and *Begonia maculata*) and starfish bromeliads (*Cryptanthus*). Variegated ivies such as *Hedera helix* 'glacier' are ideal for ground cover, as well as *Ficus pumila*. Chlorophytums, dracenas and aphelandras are ideal as larger plants to give height to the display. Among the intermediate-sized plants are peperomias (*Peperomia hederaefolia*, *P. magnoliaefolia*), and the distinctive leaf veins of fittonias (*F. argyroneura*, *F. verschaffeltii*) will add to the interest of the garden.

Among the ferns, there are many suitable subjects. The bird's nest fern (*Asplenium nidus*) is particularly attractive and the brake ferns (*Pteris*) can be had in a variety of sizes and variegations. The holly-leaf fern (*Cyrtomium falcatum*), with its glossy, dark-green, leaf-like fronds, is suitable for larger containers as it tends to be a robust grower and the maidenhair fern (*Adiantum capillus-veneris*) actually prefers being grown in a glass container.

Once you have selected the plants, you can begin assembling the garden. It is a good idea to plan the spacing of the plants beforehand on a piece of paper the same size as the area to be filled. Allow plenty of space for growth so no overcrowding occurs. Prepare the plants for insertion by gently removing most of the soil from around the roots. Work from the outside edges of the container towards the centre, using a spoon (attached to a bamboo cane if necessary) to make planting holes in the soil. Use a bamboo tweezer for small plants and a hooked wire for larger ones. Spread out the roots of each plant with a fork and then cover them with the soil. An empty wooden cotton reel attached to a bamboo stick can be used for tamping down the soil around each plant.

When the planting is complete, pour in enough water to moisten the growing medium, but not to saturate it. Replace the lid, and put the container in a slightly shaded, warm place. Condensation will probably form within a few days at the top of the bottle or tank; if none appears, add a little more water. If, on the other hand, there is so much condensation that the glass is obscured, remove the lid or stopper for a few days. Once a state of equilibrium has been reached, water the plants every few months and then only sparingly. Regular removal of all dead and dying leaves is an essential task, as fungal infections can rapidly reduce a bottle garden to an untidy mess of rotting foliage.

When filling a bottle garden, use a funnel and tube to keep the glass from becoming soiled by compost or grit.

After choosing suitable plants, gently insert them into the growing medium with a bamboo tweezer or hooked wire.

Water moderately after planting and replace the lid. Below: an imaginative grouping of bottle gardens.

Hanging baskets

It was not really practicable to grow plants in hanging baskets indoors before the advent of baskets with built in drip trays. Now, however, many plants that are best displayed in hanging baskets can be easily accommodated indoors. Baskets can be placed anywhere — on walls, hanging from rafters, in front of windows or above the centre of a doorway. Make sure when selecting a position that it is high enough not to be a hazard to the tall and yet low enough to be reached for watering and other maintenance. As a rule, baskets which are planted for seasonal display and hung outdoors should be tightly packed with a variety of plants, while those grown indoors on a more permanent basis should contain one species only, for ease of management, and be planted rather sparingly, to allow room for growth.

Hanging baskets come in a small range of sizes and are either round or semi-circular in shape. They are usually made of strong wire which is often plastic-coated or else entirely of a strong polythene. Other containers can be used, such as clay or terra cotta pots or oil cans, but the latter will need very thorough cleaning before planting. Also, drainage holes must be punched in the bottom to release excess water.

All containers must be hung from reliable supports strong unrusted chains or cables are best and rope should be avoided as it tends to stretch and rot. The fixing point for the complete basket should be a secure hook fitted into a sturdy base, such as a solid rafter, brick (not mortar) or onto a solid metal railing. If the basket is grown near a single light source, the hook should be able to be turned by a quarter daily so that all plants get equal exposure to light.

Before filling the basket, make sure it is resting on a firm base; a big flower pot or bucket is suitable. If the basket has open lattice sides, line it with sphagnum moss. Lay the moss in a thick even sward with no thin patches and do not attempt to cover more than the bottom third of the basket. Alternatively, use heavygrade black horticultural polythene. When using polythene, cut and tuck it neatly in around the top edge of the basket and make a few drainage holes in the base.

After the lining has been fixed, fill the basket by one third with good compost and firm it down gently, to avoid the completed level sinking dramatically after the first watering. Begin adding the plants; if plastic is used as a liner, cut slits in it large enough to insert the root ball. If using sphagnum, the plant stem should rest against the moss, while the roots are in contact with the soil. Place another layer of sphagnum around the sides of the basket and proceed to fill with compost so the basket is two-thirds full. Put in a second row of plants and fill the basket with the remaining compost so that it is filled nearly to the rim. Polythene-lined baskets can have a second row of slits made and a second layer of plants inserted in the same way as the first.

When planting a hanging basket, support it in a bucket; it is generally easier to fill and plant from the bottom up.

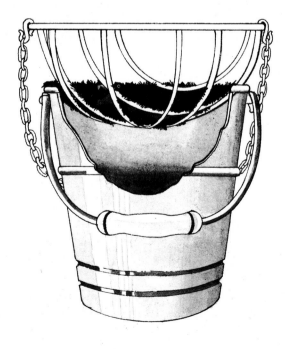

The completed basket should be well watered and allowed to settle for a couple of weeks before it is hung in its permanent position.

The type of plants grown depends very much on the amount of light available, but generally, those with a drooping or trailing habit of growth look best. In hot, sunny conditions, Christmas cactus is an excellent subject. For a less well lit spot choose from the many named varieties of ivy, philodendron or ferns.

The maintenance of hanging baskets is similar to that of pot-grown plants. Check regularly for water and give those plants which need a moist atmosphere a spray of tepid water now and again, even daily in hot dry weather. Feeding is not likely to be necessary immediately after planting; give liquid feed once the plants have settled down and are seen to be actively growing. Remove fading flowers to keep the basket attractive and also prevent energy wasted in seed formation. Remove dead and dying foliage as well, for visual reasons and also to discourage the advent of pests and diseases.

Bonsai

Although colourful packets labelled 'Bonsai seeds' are available from many garden centres and seed catalogues, this description is far more fanciful and hopeful than realistic. There is really no such thing as bonsai seed; what the packets contain is an assortment of tree seed which will produce ordinary seedlings. These can then be doctored by judicious training and pruning into bonsai trees, but it is no easy task. Many books have been written about the art of bonsai and mature specimens have changed hands for vast sums of money. Still, it is worth a try if you are intrigued by the science of controlling a tree's growth and form.

The cost of a seed packet should provide you with a reasonably interesting assortment but a quick walk through local woodlands or orchards is an equally good source. Besides the seeds themselves, young seedlings can sometimes be found growing which are dwarfed naturally or unusually shaped. Although conifers, such as pines, are excellent subjects for bonsai they are notoriously difficult to transplant. If you are attempting moving conifers take several to allow for some failures. If they are carefully lifted and potted up, an instant potential bonsai tree can be had, saving a year or two in time.

The word 'bonsai' literally means 'planted in a shallow vessel'; this practice restricts the growth of

Although they can be brought indoors for short periods of time for display, bonsai are essentially outdoor plants from the temperate zone. Without exposure to winter cold and summer heat, they would be unable to survive.

the plant and is combined with regular root and branch-pruning to keep the tree stunted. In classical bonsai, there are a number of highly formalised styles, with the trees trained into living sculptures. The young seedlings are shaped by means of wire spiralling round the stems and branches; supple wood is necessary at this stage to avoid breakage. The Japanese highly prized mature bonsai trees which were found growing naturally, perhaps in a rock cranny or very exposed position. Infinite care is needed to successfully lift and transplant such a mature tree, which probably adds to its value.

A word of warning about bonsai trees is necessary: they are most definitely not indoor plants. As one of the main requirements for a bonsai tree is that it is slow growing, species selected are almost invariably from a temperate climate. This means that they actually need exposure to the elements, the winter cold and the summer sun, to survive and they would quickly succumb to the warm, dry conditions indoors. Although a bonsai tree can be brought indoors for short periods of time, as a temporary decorative feature, it is essentially an outdoor plant.

Hydroponics

In recent years there has been a marked increase in the number of hydroponic growing kits available from florists and garden centres. Although many nurserymen have given their own trade names to hydroponic growing systems, they are actually all very similar. The first requirement is a watertight container of sufficient depth to accommodate the pot in which the plant is growing and enough inert clay granules for placing around the roots of the plant The granules are manufactured from treated clay and are very porous, absorbing about one-third of their own weight in water. Besides the container and the expanded granules, a water-level indicator is necessary to ensure that the correct water level is maintained and that there is never more than 7.5cm (3in) around the bottom of the pot. The container is filled to this maximum depth and is allowed to drop to the minimum mark on the indicator before refilling. It is essential that the indicator should remain at minimum for at least five days before refilling; this allows for the maximum amount of air to circulate around the roots of the plant. In cold weather, make sure you use tepid water and fill the container to the half-way, rather than the full mark.

The last factor is nutrient for the plant, as neither the water nor the clay particles provide any sort of food. A special fertilizer has been developed for hydroponic growing and it allows the plant to draw in as much nutrient as it requires. The problem of over-fertilizing the plant doesn't arise, although care

must be taken to recharge the unit when all the available nutrient has been absorbed. The time span will vary according to the size of the container but it is usually at six-month or yearly intervals. A hydroponic unit will have complete cultural instructions attached and if they are followed, you should have no trouble growing first-class healthy plants. One word of advice: if you are growing a group of plants in a large container with one indicator serving all the plants, it is essential that all the plant pots in the container are the same depth.

A cut-away section through a hydroponic container showing the inner container, expanded clay particles and indicator.

An Illustrated Guide To
Indoor Plants

For convenience, the illustrated guide to indoor plants has been divided into five separate categories – flowering plants, bulbs and corms, foliage plants, ferns, and cacti and succulents. Each entry has been made alphabetically under its Latin name within these divisions. For common names refer to the index on page 120.

Botanical names

Latin plant names can be a bit overwhelming, particularly to the amateur grower. Over the years, common names have been given to many popular plants to avoid dealing with Latin nomenclature. Common names, although useful enough in their own way, are often confusing and can be very misleading. For example, 'Mother of thousands' and 'Strawberry begonia' are both common names for the same plant. To make matters worse, this particular plant, *Saxifraga sarmentosa*, is neither a strawberry nor a begonia, so instead of simplifying matters, the common name has actually added to the confusion.

Latin names, on the other hand, are universally accepted, and do not vary at all, even from country to country. Besides identifying a particular plant, the complete name will also tell you about the family to which this plant belongs. The names are organized as follows: The first part of a plant's botanical name is the name of the genus, that is, the group to which the plant is related in sharing certain characteristics, particularly of its flowering parts. The genus *Ficus*, for example, includes the plants commonly called figs or rubber plants. The second part is the specific name, that is, in the case of the genus *Ficus*, the name which distinguishes one species of fig from another. Therefore, the creeping fig is *Ficus pumila*, the India rubber plant is *Ficus elastica*, and so on. The specific name is a descriptive one, telling either the geographical origin of the plant, something about the size and shape of the plant or its leaves or flowers or commemorating someone, perhaps the botanist who discovered it.

The genus is not the largest category in the system of classification; a number of related genera make up a family. The genus *Ficus* belongs, with a number of related genera, to the family *Moraceae* of which the mulberry is also a member. The genus is, however, the most convenient and generally accepted grouping of plants for a work of reference and it is under the name of the genus that the plants are listed in the dictionary.

Within a species, distinct variations occur. Some of these happen naturally, in which case a varietal name is added, also in italics, to the specific name (for example, *Ficus pumila minima*). Where varieties have arisen in cultivation they are known as cultivars and are indicated in botanical classification by the addition of a cultivar name in single quotes and in roman type after the specific name (for example, *Ficus nipponica* 'Variegata').

Besides natural varieties and cultivars many plants in cultivation are hybrids, that is crosses between species of the same genus, or more rarely, between species in related genera. Hybrids between species in the same genus are written with the name of the genus followed by a multiplication sign and the hybrid name (for example, *Camellia* × *williamsii*). In the case of a hybrid genus, the multiplication sign precedes the genus (for example, × *Fatshedera*, a cross between *Fatsia japonica* and *Hedera helix*, common ivy).

Ficus radicans, one of the ornamental figs, belongs to the same genus as the hardy, edible fig, Ficus carica, and the ornamental rubber plant, Ficus robusta. The specific name, radicans, gives a more detailed botanical description and refers, in Latin, to its ability to produce aerial roots.

FLOWERING PLANTS

Most garden plants are grown for the beauty of their flowers. Indoors, however, foliage plants are becoming increasingly popular. In many rooms, especially those with a low amount of light, the latter are far more suitable and it is better to have a thriving foliage plant than a miserable plant which may even refuse to flower.

Yet, all things having been considered, there is nothing remotely comparable to the attraction of a flower. On the purely botanical level, its structural intricacy is fascinating, but more than that, it has acquired symbolic connotations of fertility, love, success and beauty. The bouquets of flowers presented to visiting royalty, VIPs and actresses on opening nights would not seem right if they contained foliage alone, no matter how striking, colourful or fragrant the leaves.

In terms of longevity, flowering pot plants are certainly better value than cut flowers. Nevertheless, it is wrong to look on them simply as a long-term alternative to cut flowers. Although some easily-raised annuals and biennials, like celosia for example, suit this easy-come-easy-go approach and should be thrown away after flowering, most of the plants described in this section can be kept from season to season with a little care, especially if you have somewhere — a garden, greenhouse or spare room — in which to store them when dormant. Some evergreen flowering plants do not even have to be stored and will provide flowers in season and attractive foliage the rest of the year.

A major factor with flowering plants is light; good light is needed if the flowers are to open properly. Most will flower admirably on a well-lit window-sill and artificial light can be used to supplement natural light. The amount of heat needed, however, varies. The majority of spring-flowering plants, including favourites such as primula and cyclamen, require cool, airy conditions, but species from tropical climates, such as saintpaulia, require more heat. Although many flowering houseplants bloom in the spring or summer, a few, like poinsettia and azalea, produce flowers in the winter and others, like impatiens, flower on and off throughout the year. With careful management, therefore, you should be able to have a year-round succession of flowers indoors without resorting to the fading glory of cut flowers.

Abutilon

This is an easily grown shrub with pendulous, bell-shaped flowers and many species have the added attraction of variegated leaves. The leaves are maple-shaped, hence the common name, flowering maple. The best known variety, *A. striatum thompsonii*, has mottled green and yellow foliage and orange flowers marked with crimson veins.

They grow strongly in a rich compost, and they should be pruned back in February if getting too large and lanky. Cool, light conditions and a temperature of around 13-15°C (55-60°F) are suitable, with liberal watering and feeding while the shrub is actively growing but less at other times. They enjoy a spell outdoors in summer, if given a sunny sheltered site.

New plants can be raised either from seeds or from cuttings. Seeds should be sown in February in a heated greenhouse or propagator at 18°C (35°F). However, because most common varieties are hybrids, the quality of plants grown from seed is uncertain. Therefore, if you want to reproduce a favourite plant, you would do better to take cuttings from old wood in early spring or autumn. These root easily at 20°C (65°F), and if started in early spring, the plant should be mature enough to give flowers the following autumn.

Aeschynanthus lobbianus

Bearing clusters of deep red, tubular flowers in the leaf axils or at the tips of long trailing stems in summer, these are ideal plants for hanging baskets. In their native tropical environment they are epiphytic, growing in the branches of trees and the stems can reach a length of 60cm (2ft) or more. They require shade, free watering in summer, a little less in winter and temperatures of around 15-18°C (60-65°F) to thrive. You may be tempted to neglect them, however, as the leaves, normally green, become a very attractive burgundy colour when the plants are kept a little on the dry side. Additionally, excessive water tends to inhibit the production of flowers, and it is sometimes preferable to spray the leaves daily with tepid water rather than constantly water the roots. Use a free-draining compost and keep the roots relatively pot-bound to encourage flowering.

New plants can be raised from 7.5cm (3in) stem cuttings taken in summer, or from seed collected from the attractive dark pods which form after flowering is over.

Allamanda

A warm, humid atmosphere is essential for this exotic South American climbing plant, and it will only thrive with summer temperatures of about 18°C (65°F), a minimum winter temperature of 13°C (55°F) and frequent watering and feeding when in full growth. If all this can be arranged, the large, yellow, bell-shaped flowers may make the effort worthwhile. Nevertheless, only the tamer *A. neriifolia* tolerates room conditions; the more spectacular *A. cathartica* needs a greenhouse for its rampant climbing growth, which may reach a height of 5m (15ft) or more.

Cuttings need a minimum temperature of 21°C (70°F) to root and propagation is probably beyond the scope of all but the most dedicated amateur.

Anthurium scherzerianum

Whether you will want to grow this plant depends on whether you like its spectacular and unusual appearance. It is certainly distinctive, having a flower composed of a brilliant red leaf-like bract, or spathe, with a large central projecting flower spike or spadix.

It prefers a warm room, around 18°C (65°F), some shade and a humid atmosphere. It will do particularly well if you submerge the pot in a container of moist peat or moss. Try to keep the soil moist but well-drained; should you need to repot at any time, use a compost containing plenty of sphagnum moss and leaf mould and put several crocks in the bottom of the spot to ensure perfect drainage. Feed regularly with weak fertilizer.

The easiest way to raise new plants is from seed in a heated propagator; alternatively, divide the crowns in spring and pot up the sections individually.

Anthurium scherzerianum, the flame plant. Being tropical, it does best in warm, humid and slightly shady conditions.

Left: Aphelandra squarrosa, the zebra plant, gets its common name from the attractively variegated leaves. Opposite: Beloperone guttata, the shrimp plant, has curious, shrimp-like bracts but rather dull foliage and an awkward, ungainly habit of growth.

Aphelandra

It seems amazing that the large aphelandras, or zebra plants, once so popular, have now almost completely disappeared. Erstwhile popular varieties, like *A. squarrosa 'Louisae'*, are now difficult to find; the only common variety nowadays being the more compact, though less attractive, *A. squarrosa dania*. This is a favourite among commercial growers because it takes up less valuable greenhouse space. The yellow and red bracts, on which appear tubular yellow flowers, are produced in the autumn, but these are not the only feature of the plant; the shiny, variegated leaves are an equal attraction.

Aphelandras need ample water, heavy feeding, good light and a temperature in the region of 18°C (65°F). After flowering, you should cut the plants back to two sound leaves. New shoots will grow from the axils of these in the spring. You can then either leave them to grow on as they are, the simplest method, but one which does not produce the best-shaped plants, or remove them as cuttings and propagate two new plants. Put the cuttings in pure peat in a propagator at 18°C (35°F).

Azalea indica

In full flower, the azalea must be one of the most attractive of all flowering plants; purchased with lots of buds and some flowers already open, it is the easiest of plants to manage. Nevertheless, many people fail by giving insufficient water, the result being shrivelled flowers followed by the general decline of the plant.

To water an azalea bush effectively, grasp the pot in both hands, put your thumbs over the soil in the pot and submerge it in a bucketfull of water until air bubbles stop appearing. If the plants are kept watered in this way and placed in a cool room at about 13–15°C (55–60°F), there should be no difficulty. Whether rain or tap water is used makes no difference whatsoever, despite all that is written about the essential need for soft water.

As the flowers die, pick them off. Do this very carefully, because if the young growing shoot immediately below the flower is damaged, the number of flowers produced in the following season will be reduced. When all the flowers have gone, the plants can be kept quite happily outdoors. If the pots have moist peat mounded up round them and are then placed in a shaded place in the garden, this is ideal. The peat around the plants keeps the roots moist, but a regular spraying of the foliage is also appreciated. Moderately low temperatures will not affect the plants while they are resting, but they must be brought indoors if there is a likelihood of a frost.

The plants will need potting after their first year and about every two-to-three years after that. Use a rich peaty mixture with a good amount of well-rotted leaves worked into it. Propagating new plants is not easy, and is best left to the professionals.

Begonia

If you want to specialize in just one family of plants, you could not do much better than begonias. There is no end of choice, from the compact, fibrous-rooted and the more majestic tuberous-rooted varieties, both grown for their flowers, to the rhizomatous types, such as *B. rex*, grown for their foliage. If you wish, you can have flowering begonias throughout the year.

All begonias need good light and an average temperature of around 15°C (60°F) to do well. Keep roots reasonably moist and feed regularly once the plants are established. Cultivation over the dormant period depends on the type of begonia you are growing. Tuberous-rooted begonias are dealt with on

page 75 and only fibrous-rooted varieties will be considered here. Of these, one of the most popular is *Begonia semperflorens*, available with red, pink or white flowers and bright green or bronze foliage. It is easily raised from seed sown in the spring and it is not difficult to grow indoors on a light and sunny window-ledge.

Pick off old flowers when they die and after flowering, either throw the plants away — the second season's growth is never as good — or cut them back to about 15cm (6in) from soil level and keep for another season. Keep them on the dry side during the dormant period until new growth appears. They can then be repotted in a rich, peaty mixture.

Begonia 'Fireglow' (*B.* 'Reiger') is another fibrous-rooted variety and has become increasingly popular in the last few decades. By controlling the amount of light these plants are given, growers are able to produce flowering plants throughout the year, although they are most common in late spring, sum-

mer and early autumn. They have large, single orange flowers that appear over many months.

Like *B. semperflorens*, they can be cut back after flowering and kept for the following season.

Beloperone guttata

Beloperone is a greedy plant, which you will have to feed generously and pot on into a rich mixture at least once a year if you wish it to grow successfully. It is grown for its orange-yellow bracts, said to resemble shrimps and hence its common name, shrimp plant. Its red, purple or blue flowers are small and insignificant and its foliage is dull, and duller still if feeding is neglected. Nevertheless, given adequate feeding and dryish root conditions in the winter, it is not too difficult to grow if positioned in a reasonably warm and light spot. It can be pruned back to a better shape any time it gets leggy. New plants can be successfully raised from cuttings provided a minimum temperature of 21°C (70°F) is given.

Bougainvillea

Bougainvilleas are brilliant-flowering, South American shrubs with vigorous growth which nevertheless can be controlled by the careful use of supporting canes. The flowers are small and insignificant, but the surrounding bracts provide splashes of yellow, pink, orange or purple for much of the spring and summer. Its common name, paper flower, comes from the thin, papery texture of the bracts.

They are not particularly difficult, but respond best to full sunlight and careful watering. In particular, the roots must be kept moist while the plants are actively growing, although in the autumn the soil should be allowed to dry out and the plants kept dry over the winter. In this dormant stage, they will survive temperatures as low as 7°C (45°F). In the spring, repot them into a fresh, rich mixture that is on the heavy side, and resume watering. Cuttings of old wood root fairly easily in a warm propagator.

Brunfelsia calycina

This is a free-flowering plant with fragrant purple

flowers much in evidence from spring to early autumn. It does not grow large, but should be pruned back after flowering to maintain an attractive shape. If growing strongly, it will also need potting on into a rich mixture every other year. Keep the roots moist while the plants are growing strongly, but give less water through the winter months.

New plants can be propagated from cuttings of half-ripened wood, about 8cm (3in) long, at any time during the summer. You may have trouble with whitefly. Look on the underside of leaves and if you see any, treat the problem immediately.

Calceolaria

As a houseplant, calceolaria is normally treated as a biennial. Not everyone likes its strange pouch or slipper-like flowers, but if you do, try to obtain seed of one of the many modern hybrids, which are far more compact and free-flowering than older varieties. Sow the seed in early or mid-June on a layer of fine, damp sand spread over potting compost in a seed tray. Then, as the plant does not like too much light, place the tray in a shaded part of your greenhouse or in a north-facing frame. After germination,

pot the seedlings into individual pots and place these in a moderately shaded and airy part of the greenhouse. The young plants should then be ready for moving indoors in the following spring.

Once indoors, they require a light position, moderate watering and occasional feeding. When they finish flowering, usually by October, discard them. If you do not have a greenhouse or conservatory in which to grow plants from seed, you can obtain commercially raised plants in the summer in which they will flower.

Camellia

These hardy evergreen shrubs, with glossy leaves and single or double, wax-like flowers, are usually planted outdoors, but they are just as attractive indoors. Here they require cool conditions and appreciate a window position. Keep them moist, but do not overwater. If you repot them, use porous compost.

In the summer, place them outdoors in a lightly shaded position; they can be brought back indoors for the autumn, winter and spring when they flower.

You can try raising new plants from cuttings taken in mid-summer and placed in a water propagator; but be warned — they are not easy to root.

Campanula isophylla

Purchase one of these with clean, undistorted foliage and you will enjoy a continuous summer display of flowers. You will do less well with unhealthy plants distorted by virus, to which they are very prone, and which, like all virus diseases, cannot be cured.

Pick the flowers off as they die to encourage further flowers. Then, when they are finished, cut the plants back quite severely and keep them on the dry side in a frost-free place until new growth appears in the spring. You should then repot them into a rich mixture, carefully shaking off much of the old soil as you do so, and gradually give them more water.

Campanulas enjoy a well-lit position and rich soil and they are one of the easiest houseplants to grow — they flourish outside in moderate southern areas. Propagate new plants from cuttings taken in the spring. Select a new shoot with a few leaves attached and root it in a heated propagator.

Celosia argentea

The forms Cristata and Pyramidalis are cheap and cheerful annuals that come in many garish shades of red, orange and yellow and are raised from seed sown in a heated propagator in the spring. Their common name, cock's comb, refers to the curious, crest-like flower formations. Pot on plants first into 7.5cm (3in) pots and then into 15cm (6in) pots. Finally, move them into a well-lit position with a temperature of about 15°C (60°F). Avoid overwatering once they are established and feed well once in flower. After flowering, discard them.

Chrysanthemum

Everyone takes potted chrysanthemums for granted, but in fact their production from cuttings requires considerable skill and equipment and is best left to the expert. Nevertheless, they make excellent houseplants when purchased, flowering for six full weeks, given sufficient light and provided the day-time temperature is not allowed to rise above 15°C (60°F). Higher temperatures mean a shorter flowering time. When they have finished flowering, they can either be planted out in the garden, or thrown away.

When buying, never select plants that are too backward. They may never produce a full quota of flowers.

Cineraria

Cinerarias are closely related to common groundsel, *Senecio vulgaris*, and botanically the name *Senecio cruentus* is more correct than *Cineraria*. Nevertheless, the older name seems to have stuck.

Whatever the name, they are attractive potplants which give few problems if kept in a cool, light position sheltered from direct sunlight. Keep them moist, but do not overwater. Discard them once they have flowered.

If you have a frame or greenhouse, it is very easy to raise cineraria from seed. Sow in early April for winter flowering and in June for flowering the following summer. As they become established, gradually pot the plants on from trays to 7.5cm (3in) pots and finally to 13cm (5in) pots.

Clerodendrum thomsonae

These are vigorous evergreen shrubs, producing colourful clusters of red and white bracts throughout the summer. Even when confined to a 30cm (12in) pot they will grow as high as 3m (10ft), producing a magnificent spectacle if you have the space.

Keep them on the dry side during the winter, but water frequently at other times. They like a rich soil, so feed regularly during the summer and use a rich, fairly heavy compost when potting on. For the best results, try to maintain a temperature of about 18°C (65°F).

During the winter, the plants may drop leaves but do not worry, as this is quite natural and new leaves will grow in the spring. New plants can be raised from firm, young cuttings taken in spring. Insert them in small pots of a peat and sand mixture, and place them in a heated propagator.

Columnea × banksii

These pendulous evergreen sub-shrubs, with their hooded scarlet flowers look at their best when grown at head height in a hanging basket. Give them a warm (18°C, 65°F) spot, out of direct sunlight, keep them moist and apply liquid fertilizer when they are producing new growth. Cuttings root readily at any time in a heated propagator. You can put several cuttings in one pot for a more attractive plant. As the plants get bigger, repot as necessary using a rich peaty compost.

Columnea × banksii flowers in the early summer. If you want earlier flowering, try *C. crassifolia* 'Firecracker'. This has more upright foliage and flowers in the early spring.

Crossandra

The only variety of crossandra that can be purchased at all frequently is *Crossandra infundibuliformis* 'Mona Wallhed', which has orange flowers and is much more appealing than its name suggests. It has dark green, glossy leaves and bears its flowers on long spikes. It needs a warm light spot with a minimum temperature of 18°C (65°F) but does not like direct sunlight.

Mature plants produce young shoots from the

base. Cuttings taken from these can be rooted in a peat and sand mixture in a heated propagator to give new plants. When rooted, pot them on into a rich peaty compost.

Cyclamen persicum

Some people are never successful with cyclamens, yet they are not difficult to grow. A light windowsill in a coolish room — 13°C (55°F) is quite enough — is ideal for them. They are certainly worth the effort, being one of the most beautiful of all flowering pot plants, and in cool conditions they will continue to produce flowers for many months.

Watering is where many people go wrong. They should be watered and then allowed to dry out appreciably — but never bone dry — before watering again. This is far more important than how you water, often a controversial point. In fact, whether you water from the top or from the bottom makes little difference. But when watering from the top, make sure that the spout of the watering can is directed into the pot and no water splashes leaves and flowers. Water lying between the leaves and flower stalks at the bottom of the corm can result in botrytis and other fungal problems. The best remedy, should this happen, is to immediately dust the affected area with a suitable fungicide.

When the flowers die off, remove them completely, stalk and all, by pulling the stalks sharply away from the corm. Any pieces that remain are likely to rot and damage healthy flowers and leaf stalks. At the end of the season, when flowers and foliage begin to die down, let the soil gradually dry out until it is quite dry, and then remove all dead flowers and leaves. The plant can then be kept in a dry and frost-free place until the following mid-summer when new growth should have begun. When this starts, remove the plant from its pot, shake off the old soil, and repot

Cyclamen persicum, one of the most popular indoor plants, is often used for Christmas decoration. It may prove disappointing in warm, centrally-heated rooms and a cool hall or bedroom is more suitable. Although many people discard a cyclamen pot plant when the number of flowers begins to diminish and the leaves begin to yellow, it is actually a perennial corm which will flourish for many years if given an annual period of dormancy. Colours range from white through pale pink to deep rose and crimson and many forms have particularly beautiful silver-variegated leaves.

it in a fresh, rich peaty compost. The plant can then be placed in a cool, light place as before, to begin flowering again.

New plants can be raised from seeds sown in a propagator in August. Give them a temperature of 21°C (70°F) to start with, to encourage quick germination. After germination, a temperature of 15°C (60°F) is sufficient. When large enough to handle, pot the seedlings into smaller pots, and then ever larger ones as they grow bigger.

Dipladenia rosea

This is a rampant evergreen climbing plant which is not easy to manage indoors as it needs a strong system of support on which to climb, a minimum temperature of 18°C (65°F), a peaty growing mixture and constant care to ensure that watering is done only in moderation — both excessive watering and dry conditions are lethal. Less water should be given during the winter and frequent applications of weak fertilizer during the growing season is the best way of feeding.

To produce new plants, 10cm (4in) cuttings should be taken from the side shoots produced by the main stem. They can then be rooted in a heated propagator at a temperature of 21°C (70°F).

Euphorbia pulcherrima

Although better known as poinsettia, the Christmas flower should more correctly be called *Euphorbia pulcherrima*. It was originally a native of Mexico, but today's pot plants bear only a passing resemblance to the taller, coarser wild plants. In particular, growers treat their plants with growth-retarding chemicals to make them smaller and more manageable. These artificial hybrids normally have six to ten flowering bracts and are little more than 50cm (20in) tall.

Try to buy a plant at the beginning of its flowering cycle — look to see if the small flowers at the centre of the large bracts have opened or not — so that it lasts at least a month before the bracts and leaves start to fall. Obviously, the plants will survive longer the better the growing conditions. Try to put them in a spot where they will receive maximum light and a temperature of around 15°C (60°F). Avoid excessive watering and add a little liquid fertilizer each time the plant is watered.

After the bracts have fallen, you can either throw the plants away, or grow them on for another year. Getting them to produce bracts for a second time, however, is a vexing problem. In fact, many people emphatically say that it is impossible for the average householder to get flowers a second time, but this is simply not so. The important factor is artificial light. Bracts are only produced if the plants are not exposed to artificial light from late summer through to Christmas. If they are, they produce new leaves instead of bracts.

If you are going to keep a poinsettia for another year, cut it down to about 10cm (4in), and then store it in a dry and warm place, giving it just a little moisture. As soon as it starts into new growth, around April, gradually give it more water. Soon after this, either pot it on into a new pot, or repot it in its old pot after shaking away as much of the old mixture as possible without damaging the roots. Repot using a rich peaty mixture. If you would rather not persevere with an old plant, take 15cm (5in) cuttings from young shoots about 25cm (10in) long. They will root fairly easily in small pots of peat/sand mixture at 21°C (70°F).

Exacum affine

With its compact habit, glossy green leaves and pleasantly scented, blue gentian-like flowers, this is an attractive annual for indoor growing. Sow the seeds at 21°C (70°F) in the spring and then grow the plants at a slightly lower temperature in a lightly shaded spot. Keep moist and feed occasionally. Flowering will continue for six to eight weeks; once flowering is over, the plant should be discarded.

Fuchsia

If you want to grow these generally outdoor shrubs indoors, give them the lightest spot possible as poor light will inevitably result in premature loss of flowers. Keep the roots moist while the plants are actively growing and feed frequently. Warmth, however, is not needed, 15°C (60°F) being ideal. After flowering, prune the plants back hard, and keep them on the dry side in a frost-free place until the following spring. They can then be started into growth by immersing the pots in a bucket of water, thoroughly soaking the rootball. If pot-bound, they should be potted on into a larger pot containing a rich peaty compost, once growth has started. Cuttings can be propagated with little difficulty at any time of the year except mid-winter. Alternatively you can sow seed collected from the berries which follow the flowers in late autumn, but the seedlings will be of mixed quality.

Gardenia jasminoides

Producing double, creamy-white flowers with a heady fragrance which fills the house, gardenias must have cool, light conditions to be successful. It is best to use a lime-free compost and water with lime-free

Exacum affine, or Persian violet, is a sweet-scented annual, and is actually closely related to gentians, not to violets.

water. The presence of lime turns the leaves a chlorotic yellow. If your plants suffer from this, treat the soil with sequestrine of iron. Keep the roots moist, but make sure the pots are well drained.

New plants can be produced from 8cm (3in) shoot cuttings inserted in a peat and sand mixture in the early spring and kept in a heated propagator until the cuttings have rooted.

Heliotropium × *hybridum*

These fragrant, multipurpose plants, commonly called cherry pie, do well in a cool greenhouse, out-doors in the garden in the summer, or as pot plants on a light window-ledge. As pot plants, however, they grow too vigorously if left to themselves, so prune overgrown plants back hard in the early spring and, if you want a bushy plant, pinch out the growing points in February or March as well. Keep the soil

moist and feed regularly while the plants are actively growing.

Any healthy trimmings cut during pruning can be used to raise new plants. Cut them to 7.5cm (3in) long and root them in a peat and sand mixture in a heated propagator. Alternatively, you can raise new plants with seeds sown in the spring.

Hibiscus rosa-sinensis

It is not surprising that hibiscus, or 'rose mallow', has become increasingly popular, as this obliging tropical plant will produce flowers for months on end during the summer. The individual flowers may only last a day, but new flowers open all the time. You have a choice of many different brilliant colours, including red, yellow, orange and pink. For a moder-ately vigorous plant, temperature is not important, anything between 15–20°C (60–70°) is suitable. They

Right: Gardenia jasminiodes, or Cape jasmine, is exquisitely scented and its flowers were much prized by Victorians for wearing in button holes. It has a reputation for being a difficult plant to grow and one which drops its buds at the first sign of discontent. Given an even, moderate temperature, a moist atmos-phere and a continual supply of water in the growing season, it will thrive and produce its showy white flowers, up to 5 cm (2 in) across, through summer and well into autumn.
Opposite: Hibiscus rosa-sinensis, or rose mallow. If planted out in the greenhouse border, it can reach a height of 1.8 m (6 ft) or more, but it is equally happy when grown in a moderate-sized pot.

will tolerate winter temperatures as low as 10°C (50°F). They do like a bright, airy position, however. If you can provide enough heat and light you can get flowers all the year round. Otherwise you may have to move the plants out of your living room once flowering is over, as, although they are evergreen, their foliage is not particularly attractive.

Do not feed, and water only scarcely, during the winter when the plants are not blooming; feed weekly and water liberally — never letting the roots dry out — in the summer.

With care, you may be able to raise new plants from cuttings, but do not be disappointed if you fail, as they are not easy to root. Only warm and moist conditions in a heated propagator will suffice and it is usually best left to experts.

Hoya carnosa

This rampant evergreen climber needs a rich, heavy mixture and a pot of at least 30cm (12in) diameter if it is to do well. It also needs good light, ample feeding in the growing season and a summer temperature of around 16°C (60°F), although it will survive a temperature of 7°C (45°F). Water when the rootball is dry in summer and very sparingly in the winter.

The foliage is attractive and this is complemented by the exquisite waxy, pink or white flowers, which hang down in clusters. Because of this, the plant looks its best in a hanging basket, or trained across the roof of a conservatory, for example. Never remove the flower stalks after flowering as next year's flowers will be produced at the end of these old stalks.

New plants are easy to produce. You can either root 5cm (2in) long cuttings in a heated propagator or raise new plants by layering. To do this, peg down young shoots into sandy peat in the summer, and then separate them from the parent plant when they have successfully rooted.

Hydrangea hortensis

These deciduous flowering shrubs are one of the most popular pot plants, probably because they do not require great heat. Normal room temperature is fine when they are growing and flowering in the spring and summer, while in the winter, established plants can be stood outside in a sheltered position in all but the coldest areas.

Indoors, plants should be watered and fed generously during the growing season, as hydrangeas abhor dry roots. A light position is also preferable.

The easiest thing to do with the shrub when it has finished flowering is to cut out most of the old wood — leaving only new shoots coming from the base of

the plant, and then to place the hydrangea outdoors. You can then safely ignore it, unless there is a particularly heavy frost, in which case it should be brought indoors.

The normal practice is to bring hydrangeas indoors when new leaf buds appear in the early spring. Alternatively, you can force them into early growth by bringing them into a warm greenhouse in the late winter.

Cuttings of shoots, with two pairs of leaves, taken in the spring root easily in gentle heat, and should be big enough to be potted into their final 13cm (5in) pots at the end of the summer. For the best results, use a heavy, well-drained potting mixture.

Growers offer hydrangeas in various shades of pink, blue and white. The white variety cannot be altered, but pink flowers can be turned blue by adding aluminium — in the form of aluminium sulphate 20g (¾oz) per pot — to the soil. Conversely, blue varieties will turn pink if grown in an alkaline soil, as this will make less aluminium available to the plant.

Impatiens sultanii

Busy lizzie is an old favourite, both because it flowers almost the whole year round and because it is so easy to grow and propagate. And now many new hybrids have been produced with more richly coloured flowers and darker, less insipid foliage.

If kept moist, well fed and in good light but with a little shade from the hottest summer sun, impatiens grow rampantly. Untidy plants can be pruned at any time, and the cuttings used for propagation.

Avoid excessively high temperatures — and watch for aphids on young shoots. If you see any, treat them with insecticide, but do not use malathion, as this will damage the plant.

If you have never grown a plant from cuttings, impatiens is the one to start with. Cuttings root remarkably easily in a jar of water or any ordinary compost. Keep the compost fairly dry until rooting has taken place, and then gradually increase the amount of water given.

Jasminum polyanthum

This is an exceptionally beautiful but vigorous climber which makes a difficult subject for a pot plant in a confined space and it needs severe pruning every autumn if it is to be kept within bounds. A stout framework is also needed to support the heavy mass of growth it produces. Keep the plants in a cool spot and make sure they get plenty of light. The plants should be kept quite dry during the winter and even when the plant is growing and flowering it should never be watered too frequently.

A well-grown plant produces clusters of heavily scented white flowers in the spring. As a rule plants that are too generously fed and overpotted tend to produce fewer blooms, although the delicate, fern-like foliage is quite attractive in itself. After flowering, you can nip back new growth ruthlessly and then repot the plants in June in fresh compost. It is a good idea to give them a spell outdoors in the summer, to ripen off new growth. By the end of autumn, new flower buds should be apparent and if the plants are then brought inside flowers will be produced in late winter or early spring.

Unless you have a greenhouse, it is not really worth trying to get a second crop of flowers from a potted jasmin. It is, however, very easy to grow new plants from cuttings taken from partially ripe wood in spring and thus you can have a continual supply of new plants.

Medinilla magnifica

Do not try and grow medinilla if you cannot provide an exacting regime of high temperature (at least 20°C, 70°F) and high humidity. But if you can, these

Hypocyrta glabra

This is a neat plant with glossy, fleshy green leaves and small, but attractive, orange and scarlet flowers produced over a long season. It is not particularly easy, disliking both dry conditions and overwatering, and it does best in a light position with shade from direct sunlight. It should be fed during the spring and summer, with dilute liquid fertilizer.

To raise new plants, take cuttings from the top growth of the old plant, remove the bottom one or two leaves and insert the cuttings into a mixture of peat and sand in a heated propagator.

exotic plants are well worthwhile. They grow to a height of 1m (3ft), a similar spread, and have pendulous clusters of attractive pink flowers, with large pale pink bracts, similar in shape to a hanging bunch of grapes. They need frequent syringing, ample watering and regular feeding while in active growth.

Cuttings are no easier than the mature plants. They need a high temperature inside a propagator which is itself inside a heated greenhouse.

Oxalis

Their common name, wood sorrel, makes these plants sound far too ordinary; they are pretty plants with a wide range of flower colours and attractive leaves. They are also hardy and easy to grow. Cool conditions, light shade and moderate watering are their principle requirements.

After flowering, they become dormant, losing both leaves and flowers, and during this period they should be put in a cool place and kept just moist. Bring them out again when they start into new growth.

If you want to raise new plants, they can be raised from seed, from tubers or by dividing old plant clumps.

Pachystachys lutea

The small, white, purple-tinted flowers of pachystachys or lollipop plant do not last very long, and these plants are primarily grown for the accompanying yellow bracts, which not only emerge before the flowers but also remain after they have died. When these eventually fall, however, prune the plants back to a more agreeable shape as the foliage is coarse and unattractive.

Keep pachystachys warm, feed it well, and never allow its roots to dry out. Raise new plants from cuttings with two leaves attached. These can be taken at any time of the year, provided you have a propagator in which a temperature of 18°C (65°F) can be maintained. When potting up, use a rich, heavy mixture.

Passiflora

The most common species of passion flower, *P. caerulea*, can reach some 8m (25ft) if left to grow unchecked in a greenhouse, so indoors it must be

Opposite: Pachystachys lutea, or lollipop plant, has bright yellow bracts which are attractive over much of the year.
Right: Passiflora caerulea, or passion flower, was named by missionaries in its native South America because the curious structure of the flower seemed to symbolize the passion of Christ: the three stigmas representing the three nails, the five anthers the five wounds, the ten petals the ten Apostles, and so on. Besides exquisite flowers, attractive, bright-orange, edible fruit is produced in late summer, given favourable growing conditions.

restricted. Do this by confining its roots to a small pot, which fortunately encourages more of the exotic flowers to develop. The long shoots can then be trained around a trellis of canes.

Keep the soil moist in the summer, fairly dry in winter. Prune the plants in winter, cutting back long shoots to four or five leaves. Mealy bugs are a serious pest, and the foliage should be inspected frequently. If any bugs are found, spray immediately with insecticide.

New plants can be propagated from cuttings but are probably more easily raised by layering. Simply peg down a long shoot into a peaty mixture and cut it from the parent when it has rooted.

Pelargonium

There are numerous types of pelargonium, large and small, and in a wide range of colours, but perhaps the miniatures, most suited to growing indoors, are also the most attractive. All varieties, however, are easy to grow and propagate. They are commonly called geranium which is slightly confusing as true geraniums are hardy perennial plants bearing little resemblance to pelargoniums.

They should be given as light a position as possible —placing them outdoors in a sunny location on a hot day is a good idea — watered freely while actively growing in the summer but sparingly in the winter and fed regularly in the summer.

To propagate new plants, take firm young cuttings with several leaves attached, allow the sap to dry off from the ends, and then insert them into a peat/sand mixture. When they have rooted, pot them into a well-drained mixture and pinch out the growing tips to induce more attractive, bushy plants.

Plumbago capensis

Although better suited to a large greenhouse or cool conservatory, you can, if you wish, grow these plants indoors. Trained up a frame in a light and airy place, their pale-blue, primrose-like flowers can be quite breathtakingly beautiful in mid-summer. Feed and water freely in the summer, but give less water and no fertilizer in the winter. Prune untidy growth in January, but not too severely.

New plants can be raised either from spring-sown seed or from cuttings. Both require a temperature of 21°C (70°F). Cuttings should be about 7.5cm (3in) long and can be taken at any time during the summer.

Primula

This is a large genus of over 500 plants, a few of which grow well indoors. Probably the most popular species are *P.obconica* and *P.malacoides*. *P.obconica*

has round leaves and bears its flowers, which are available in a wide range of colours, on short stems. Quite often it flowers throughout the entire twelve months of the year. It has one serious drawback however: some people with sensitive skins come out in a rash whenever they come into contact with this plant. Gloves may be an answer, but such people would do far better to grow the neater and more delicately flowered *P. malacoides*, which does not cause skin troubles.

Part of the fun of growing primulas is raising them from seed; as pot plants they are treated as annuals. The seed is very fine and should be sown on the surface of a sifted peat and sand mixture in a seed box. Cover this with glass, and place it outside until the seed germinates. The young seedlings should then be pricked out and spaced in a second box to grow on until they are big enough for planting in pots filled with a rich peaty mixture.

Throughout their lives, primulas prefer cool, moist, and lightly shaded conditions, indoors they do best in a cool room with indirect light. In addition, if at all possible, submerge the pot in a large container of damp peat or moss to keep the surrounding atmosphere moist.

Saintpaulia ionantha

The African violet is one of the most popular indoor plants, and deservedly so. Although growers have produced a wide range of named varieties, with both single and double flowers, the most common is still the original violet-blue variety with its conspicuous yellow stamens in the centre of the flowers. In good conditions, a plant will flower several times a year, including mid-winter, when it is much appreciated.

Perhaps the most fascinating thing about saintpaulias is the way they can be propagated from leaf cuttings, with a minimum of effort and a very high success rate. Although saintpaulias are easy to propagate, they are not easy to grow. To do well, they must have very good light — daylight — supplemented by artificial light in the evening is ideal — and an average temperature is of about 18°C (65°F) throughout the 24 hours of the day. Water them with tepid water only, as cold water is harmful. Add liquid fertilizer to the water while the plants are producing new flowers.

Solanum capsicastrum

It is debatable whether this plant, commonly called winter cherry, should be considered here, as its flowers are insignificant and it is grown instead for its round, shiny orange and red berries. It is usually available from December onwards. Keep it in a light, airy spot, water it well, and feed it occasionally with liquid fertilizer. The better its conditions, the longer it retains its berries.

As a houseplant, it is normally treated as an annual and is thrown away after the berries have fallen. If you want to raise your own new replacements, sow seed in early spring, and gradually pot the plants on in a richer mixture while they are still young. Give them cool, light conditions, such as a frame or unheated greenhouse. They like to be moved outdoors in the summer if the weather permits, but keep them well-watered outside, and move them indoors if it becomes unseasonably cold. Pinch out the growing tips to encourage bushy growth.

In the autumn they should be moved to their final position indoors. If kept in good conditions, the berries which are white to begin with, gradually turn red as Christmas approaches.

Spathiphyllum

This is an unusual tropical evergreen plant, which forms a cluster of glossy green, pointed leaves, some 45cm (18in) long. From the centre of the plant a tall stalk develops bearing the large, white, shield-like bract, or spathe, surrounding a poker-like spadix on which the true flowers develop; the plant's common name, white sails, refers to the appearance of the flower structure. The spathe remains attractive for several weeks and it is not unusual to have several flowers on one plant at the same time.

To do well, spathiphylums need shade and humid conditions. You will also have to feed them

Spathiphyllum, or white sails, is tropical in origin and appreciates warmth, some shade and plenty of moisture, both atmospheric and in the soil.

71

during the spring and summer, and for the best results, repot them once a year into a rich peaty mixture. Do this in the early spring before the flowers develop. New plants can be easily obtained by dividing mature plants when repotting.

Stephanotis floribunda

If you have a greenhouse or sunny ledge to which a glass frame can be fixed, it is worth trying this greenhouse climber indoors, as its waxy white flowers are both beautiful and fragrant. Unfortunately, the glossy green leaves do tend to fall during the winter, but the plants grow new foliage in the spring.

If stephanotis is trained back and forth on a supporting circular framework, its rampant upward growth can be severely curtailed, making it more manageable indoors. Nevertheless, you will have to prune established plants drastically from time to time. Keep them moist during the spring and summer, and on the dry side for the rest of the year.

New plants can be raised at any time of the year from cuttings with two leaves attached, or, if you can obtain some, from seeds. Either way you will have to be patient; both methods take a long time. When potting on, use a rich fairly heavy mixture. One problem is mealy bug, which loves getting in among the tangled foliage. Keep your eyes open for the tell-tale signs of white 'wool', and if you see any, spray with insecticide.

Streptocarpus

The hybridists have done a great deal of work on streptocarpus, or Cape primrose, in recent years, producing varieties with attractive colours, but the old blue variety Constant Nymph is still as good as any. Cultivation is easy and consists of regular watering and no feeding in the dormant winter period. However, repotting in early spring into a rich mixture will be beneficial.

Plants can be raised from seed, but propagation by leaf cuttings or division of the large old plants are easier methods. For leaf cuttings, cut a leaf into sections about 7.5cm(3in) long, and insert these into a peat/sand mixture in a moderately heated propagator.

Thunbergia alata

Free-flowering, free-climbing, but not free of pests, describes this hardy annual climber, commonly called black-eyed Susan, which produces cream and purple flowers with a black throat. Start it from seeds sown in early spring, gradually potting the plants on into a richer mixture until they are in their final 7.5cm (3in) pots. They can then be brought indoors, but you will have to provide a trellis or frame for support. Inspect them regularly for aphids and pests, and spray with insecticide if necessary. Dispose of them after flowering, as they are not worth growing on.

Streptocarpus, or Cape primrose, is South African in origin and is not related to Primula vulgaris, the primrose which grows wild in English woods and hedgerows. Although it is a long-lived perennial, older plants are particularly vulnerable to infestation by aphids and many growers treat them as annuals. Streptocarpus seeds are very fine, almost dust-like, and it is easier to propagate them from leaf cuttings; this method of propagation also ensures that the new plants will be exact replicas of the mother plant.

BULBS AND CORMS

Besides the number of tender bulbs and corms available, there are many hardy bulbs which can be forced to flower earlier indoors than they would outside. To see the first snowdrop pushing its way through the snow is a great pleasure but to see a bowl tightly packed with the same bulbs indoors on a window ledge can be equally pleasing.

Growing common garden bulbs indoors is not as simple as it may first seem. If you are using bulb fibre as a growing medium, this container must be watertight and not less than 10cm (4in) deep. You can prepare all sorts of potting mixture of your own, but it is very much simpler and usually much more satisfactory to purchase a proprietary potting mixture that has been specially prepared for growing bulbs.

Whatever type of bulb is being considered, it is important that the potting mixture should be well moistened in advance. A good guide when checking the moisture content of the compost is to compress a fistful in your hand; if water drips out freely, then it is too wet but if there is no surface water visible it is clearly much too dry. If the mixture is correctly moistened, you should just be able to squeeze moisture from between your fingers.

Immediately before planting, gently firm the mixture with your fingers. Press the bulbs into the mixture and just far enough apart for them not to touch. With smaller bulbs, such as crocus, snowdrops and grape hyacinths, the more bulbs per container the greater the display will be. Much has been said

and written about the exact planting depth for particular bulbs, but other than hyacinths, which definitely look best with their tips showing just above the surface of the compost, it is not a matter of great importance. Unless something has gone radically wrong with the preparation, the bulbs will grow and flower, given a reasonable, if imprecise, depth of soil. One of the principal reasons for bulbs producing weak and discoloured foliage or failing to flower is often the bulb itself. If you purchase very inexpensive bulbs which are pitted or otherwise marked, then poor performance will result. Large, firm, top-quality bulbs will always cost more, but the end result will bear little comparison to that of inferior bulbs.

If you have good bulbs to begin with, half the battle is won. On the other hand gross mismanagement or abysmal cultivation can counteract all the effort and money expended in getting first-quality bulbs. Having filled containers with compost and planted the bulbs, the best place for them for the following two months or so is out in the garden, where they will develop a vigorous, healthy root system. Select a cool, level and shaded spot. If you have more than one container, they should be placed close enough to touch each other. Cover the containers with 15cm(6in) of peat, sand or old bonfire ash. After six weeks outdoors, inspect the bulbs for growth. Once there is about 10cm(4in) of growth, put them in a cool, shaded cold frame or shady part of the greenhouse until the growth, which is pale, creamy white at this stage, takes on normal green colouring. In the case of miniature bulbs, however, the height will be proportionately less.

When the leaves are green, take the containers into the house and put them in a cool reasonably light place; early-flowering crocus, chionodoxa, muscari and iris should be left in the greenhouse or cold frame until the flower buds are just starting to colour. Remember to rotate the containers regularly to ensure that growth is not one-sided. Because most bulb bowls have no drainage holes, the risk of overwatering is high. A simple way of dealing with this problem is to put some pieces of broken clay flowerpot, or crocks, on one side of the container when planting. After watering, tip the bowl towards this point to dispose of surplus water.

If Christmas-flowering bulbs, such as daffodils

Left: Achimines longiflora, or hot water plant; white, scarlet and violet flowering forms are available.
Opposite: one of the many tuberous-rooted begonias available, here used to complement and enhance a subdued colour scheme indoors.

or hyacinths, are desired, it is most important that pre-cooled, treated bulbs are purchased. Bulbs which have not been treated will flower much later in the season. Once bulbs such as daffodils, tulips and hyacinths have been forced, they should be planted out in the garden and not used for forcing again, as the results will be disappointing.

Achimenes longiflora

Few plants are as colourful, or flower over such a long period, as achimenes, or hot-water plants. You have plenty of choice, too, as many different-coloured hybrids, ranging from violet or scarlet through white, can be obtained. Central American in origin, they are usually bought in early summer when in flower. If kept warm and moist and given plenty of light they will continue to flower until autumn. Being deciduous, the small toothed, dark green leaves and stems will begin to yellow and die back. Once all above ground has started to fade, gradually withold

more and more water until the root ball has dried off completely. Then store it, in its pot, in a warm, dark place until the following spring.

New plants can be started from seed, sown in a heated propagator in March, or from stem cuttings taken in April, but it is probably easiest to raise new plants from the tuber-like rhizomes which are formed on the roots of the plant. Obtain them by turning a mature plant out of its pot and carefully split them away from the parent plant. Put them 2.5cm(1in) deep in a peaty compost in early spring. Water sparingly until above-ground growth appears and then gradually increase the amount of water. To encourage bushy, well-formed plants, it is advisable to pinch off the growing tips while the plant is still young.

Begonia

Although there are many fascinating indoor begonias, only the tuberous-rooted ones are considered here;

the most popular of these is probably *B.* × *tuber-hybrida*, which has quite ordinary leaves, but enormous, rose-like flowers in a wide range of colours. *Begonia* × *tuberhybrida* 'Pendula' produces smaller flowers, but larger numbers of them, and, because of its pendulous habit of growth, looks best in hanging baskets.

New plants can be raised from very fine seed sown in early spring in a peaty mixture. The seed is almost too minute to handle and should be mixed with fine sand for even distribution and sown on the surface of the seed compost. Maintain a temperature of 18°C(65°F) until the seedlings are visible, after which it can be lowered slightly, to about 16°C (61°F). If you know someone with a tuberous begonia, you can make new plants from stem cuttings. The surest way of succeeding with tuberous begonias, however, is to buy the tubers in early spring. Start them off by pressing them into moist peat, with the top of the tuber still visible. Keep the temperature above 15°C(60°F); as soon as growth is well underway, transfer the plants to single pots filled with a slightly richer growing medium. If you are growing pendulous begonias, at the same time as you transplant them pinch out their growing points to encourage bushy growth.

Begonias have both male and female flowers growing on the same plant and it is the male flowers which are the larger and more attractive. With the large-flowered varieties, it is best to remove the small female seed flowers as soon as they appear. They are usually found under the main flower and can be identified by their winged seed pods. If these are left, the principal flowers will be greatly reduced in size.

Begonias need a lot of light to do really well and they are more at home in a greenhouse or conservatory than in dimly-lit rooms. They must be sited well away from draughts, however, to avoid bud-drop. Feed with a liquid fertilizer twice a month from the time the flower buds first appear until the flowers begin to fade. When the plant begins to die down naturally in the autumn, reduce the amount of water gradually until the tuber is ready for storage. Keep it in a warm, dry place in a box filled with dry peat or sand. To keep the tubers from completely shrivelling up, water the sand or peat sparingly. Tuberous begonias can be had in a variety of colours, ranging from white through yellows, oranges, pinks and deep reds.

Clivia miniata

This very handsome South African plant is unusual in that both the flowers and the foliage are visually striking. Often flowering bulbs have beautiful flowers for a very short period and nothing but dull foliage for the rest of the year. The reddish-orange flowers are produced in spring on the ends of a thick stem and there can be more than fifty bell-shaped flowers on a single stem. The leaves, which are strap-shaped and shiny green, last all year-round. Although there is a slow, continual replacement of old, dying leaves by new ones, the plant is never bare or unattractive.

Clivia is an undemanding plant, suitable for a warm, sunny room. It needs plenty of light, but should be sheltered from strong sunlight. A fairly rich, heavy potting mixture is best and plenty of water and liquid fertilizer should be given in the growing season. While the plant is dormant, in autumn and winter, give just enough water to keep the leaves from shrivelling.

Clivias are relatively expensive plants to buy initially but are very long-lasting and will slowly increase in size over the years. Old specimens can be magnificent, but if they get too large and begin to crack the pots they can be split up and potted into smaller containers. Clivias can be raised from seed, but these are often hard to come by and it will be a long time before plants of any substance can be expected.

Cyclamen persicum

The problem plant of many indoor growers, this is the one that never seems to do the right thing and yet for other growers it is the finest flowering plant of them all. When well grown, during the winter months of the year there are few plants that can compare with its cool beauty and elegant flowers. 'Cool' is perhaps the key word here, particularly when it comes to cultivation; in order to succeed they must not be subjected to very hot and dry conditions. A cool, light airy environment suits them best. Temperatures around 13–15°C (55–60°F), the lightest possible window ledge and plenty of fresh air should be the aim.

The watering routine is not difficult. The roots must be kept moist while the plant is actively growing. However, this does not mean total saturation and it is best to let the compost dry out a little between waterings. Should the flowers go limp as a result of too little water, do not simply fill the pot with water in an attempt to put things right as the flower stalks will simply draw water up their limp stalks and remain drooping. It is far more effective to put a few small canes in the pot and tie the flowers around them in an upright position before watering. The

Clivia miniata, or Kaffir lily, has striking, architectural foliage and is a handsome plant all-year-round.

canes can then be removed and the flower stalks will remain upright.

New plants can be raised from seed sown in a temperature of 21°C (70°F) in the autumn in full shade. Once the seeds have germinated, the seedlings can be gradually brought into light and allowed to grow on before being potted into small pots filled with a peaty mixture. Once a cyclamen has finished flowering, it can be gradually dried off and allowed to rest during the summer months; leave the corm, still in its pot, under greenhouse staging or outdoors in a cool shady place. In mid-summer, begin to encourage new growth by watering and repotting in fresh compost.

Eucharis grandiflora

Although eucharis belongs to the same family as the ordinary garden daffodil, it is very much a tropical plant needing plenty of warmth to do well. Its common name, Amazon lily, gives some indication of the growing conditions necessary. A minimum temperature of 21°C (70°F) is best. The flowers, which are creamy white and beautifully scented, are carried on stems up to 60cm (2ft) high from late summer through autumn.

For the best effect, plant several bulbs in 25cm (10in) pots filled with rich compost. Keep them moist and well fed during spring, summer and early autumn. After flowering has finished, gradually withhold water and once the bulbs have dried out store them until the following season. The plants may be propagated from seed but this is a slow process. An easier and quicker method is to remove the offsets which are formed at the bases of the bulbs and pot them up separately in summer. In any case, the Amazon lily should be repotted every third or fourth year in a fresh compost and the offsets can easily be removed at this time.

Freesia × kewensis

Freesias require relatively cool growing conditions and are really more suitable for the cool greenhouse or conservatory kept just above freezing than warm indoor rooms. In mild areas, they are often grown outdoors. You can, however, bring the plants to the flowering stage in a cool environment and then take them indoors to flower. Freesias are much loved for their exquisite scent and delicate colouring.

Most of the freesias cultivated today are hybrids developed from two fairly rare species. There are many named cultivars, with colours ranging from white through yellow, orange, red, blue and violet. The flowers are carried in spikes on thin stems up to 60cm (2ft) tall and the time of flowering is dependent on when the corms are started into growth. For flowers in mid-winter, start them in August; for flowers in April start the corms in December, and so on. Use a fairly rich potting mixture and plant several corms to a pot, 2.5cm (1in) deep and 5cm (2in) apart. Water sparingly until growth appears and then more freely. Keep them in a minimum temperature of 5°C (41°F) and once the flower buds appear give a dilute feed with liquid fertilizer every two weeks. Following flowering, gradually allow the soil to dry out. Once the plants have completely died back, remove the offsets, if you wish to propagate them, and store in cold, but frost-free, conditions until the growing process

Left: gloriosa, or glory lily, is a tropical climber which makes a superb floral display during the summer months. Opposite: gloxinias, or, more accurately, sinningias, are among the most popular and easy-to-grow indoor plants; there are many named forms available in a wide colour range.

starts again. Freesias can also be grown from seed, but it is a slow process and seedlings rarely come true. However, there is a certain amount of pleasure to be had in raising freesias from seed, as mixed strains often contain unusual new colour variations.

Gloriosa

The glory lily is aptly named, for few greenhouse plants can compare to the stunning beauty of its deep crimson, lily-like flowers which appear in succession through summer. In its native tropical Africa, it grows as a climber, scrambling through other plants and clinging by means of the hooked tendrils on the tips of the leaves. There are two species commonly grown: *Gloriosa rothschildiana*, which has rich red and yellow flowers with prominent stamens and *Gloriosa superba*, which has yellowy-orange flowers with slightly ruffled edges to the petals.

For the best effect, plant several tubers in a 25cm (10in) pot filled with rich compost in late winter or early spring. Water sparingly to begin with. However, once the plants start growing, water more frequently and give regular feeds with dilute liquid manure. Gloriosas need plenty of light and ideally should be started off in a greenhouse; if they are brought indoors to flower, put them in the sunniest possible position. Supply stakes or wires for support and once flowering has finished gradually withhold water until the plants are dry. Store the bulbs in a warm dark place until they are ready to be brought into growth the following season. If you wish to propagate them, remove the tiny offsets produced at the base of the bulbs when potting them up in spring.

Gloxinia

More properly known as *Sinningia speciosa*, gloxinias are popular and easy-to-grow indoor plants. Tuberous rooted, gloxinias produce velvety, bell-shaped

flowers in a wide range of colours; white, pink, violet and red forms are available, and there are many named varieties. Tropical in origin, gloxinias need plenty of warmth and protection from direct sunlight, a moist atmosphere and a rich, peaty soil mixture.

If you are growing them from dormant tubers, start the process in late winter by placing the tubers in boxes filled with a mixture of moist peat and sand; the temperature should be a minimum of 21°C (70°F). Once new growth has appeared, pot the tubers on into 15cm (6in) pots, putting the tuber just under the surface of the potting compost. Water frequently and once the flower buds appear, feed regularly with liquid fertilizer. After flowering, gradually withhold water and when the tubers are completely dry, store them in a warm dark place until they are started into growth the following year.

Propagation is by means of seed, division of tubers in spring or by leaf cuttings taken in summer and inserted in boxes containing a mixture of peat and sand.

Hippeastrum

Large hippeastrum bulbs have become very costly but properly prepared bulbs can provide a wonderful show of colour over a period of many years. Three or four flowers, which are trumpet shaped, are carried on thick stems up to 60cm (2ft) high. Bulbs can be had to flower in spring, summer, autumn or winter. Most hippeastrums sold today are hybrids; white, pale yellow, pink, salmon, orange and red named varieties are available, as well as striped flowers and ones with ruffled petals.

Purchase only top-quality bulbs and plant them to half their depth in pots filled with rich compost, using 17cm (7in) pots for the largest bulbs and 12cm (5in) pots for smaller bulbs. An old trick to encourage flowering is to place the bulb in warm water, or on a radiator, for several hours before planting. Water moderately until the flower spike appears and then water more freely. Keep in warm, light and dry conditions and continue to feed and water the bulb after flowering is over. The leaves will not yet be fully developed and will need the extra nutrition to continue growing and to provide essential food for the build-up of the bulb for the following season. Once the leaves start to turn yellow, gradually withhold water and stop all liquid fertilizer. When the leaves have died off completely, store the bulbs in a warm dry place for three or four months. This gives them the rest period they need after flowering and allows them to build up strength for future flowering.

The easiest way to propagate hippeastrums is by removing the offsets produced at the base of mature

bulbs and potting them on individually. You can raise hippeastrums from seed, but seedlings of hybrids will be of mixed quality.

Hyacinth

White, yellow, pink, red or blue, Dutch hyacinths are doubly attractive as indoor plants. Besides their tall, richly coloured spikes of flowers, the heady fragrance gives an added bonus. As with all bulbs used for forcing indoors at an earlier time than they would normally flower, it is essential to purchase specially prepared bulbs. Forced bulbs can be brought into flower from late autumn through late spring by exposing them to heat and light. Once bulbs have been forced into flower, they should be planted out in the garden, as they can never be forced again.

Lachenalia

Cape cowslip, as lachenalia is commonly called, is a tender, South African bulbous plant which really does best in a greenhouse, although it can be brought indoors to flower. The slender, tubular flowers appear in racemes on delicate stalks up to 30cm (1ft) high. The flowers range in colour from white through yellow, green, orange and red and many are multicoloured; winter and spring are the main flowering periods.

There are several species in cultivation and many named varieties, but they all require the same growing conditions. Plant the bulbs 2.5cm (1in) deep and 5cm (2in) apart, in pots or hanging baskets filled with a rich, well-drained compost in early autumn. Leave the pot in full sunlight and keep the temperature at a minimum of 10°C (50°F). Moisten the compost prior to planting the bulbs but do not water again until the foliage appears. From this point on, water regularly and give dilute liquid feed once every two weeks. After flowering is over, gradually withhold water until the leaves have completely died back. Leave the dormant bulbs in the pots and store in a dark dry place until the following autumn, when the bulbs should be repotted. New plants are easily obtained by dividing clumps of bulbs at this time and potting them up separately.

Lily

When about to grow lilies in pots indoors it is best to seek the advice of a specialist grower, as not all lilies are suitable for pot culture. As a general rule, stem-rooting species, such as *L. formosanum*, *L. hansonii*, *L. henryi*, *L. × hollandicum*, *L. japonicum*, *L. × maculatum*, *L. pumilum*, *L. regale* and *L. rubellum* are suitable, and also the Mid-Century Hybrids. Even then, most of the growing, up to flowering stage, is best done outdoors or in a greenhouse, with the plants brought indoors just as they are about to flower. In autumn plant the bulbs singly in 15cm (6in) pots filled with a mixture composed of equal parts of loam, peat and coarse sand. Cover the bulbs completely with the potting mixture; keep the mixture just moist and the plants in a cool place until growth is evident. Transfer the plants to a warmer location, preferably a greenhouse, and increase the

Opposite: early, mid-season and late-flowering Dutch hyacinths are available to bring colour and scent indoors for six months a year. Always pot up early-flowering bulbs first, so they have time to develop a strong roots system. Once forced hyacinths have finished flowering, harden them off gradually and then plant them out into the garden, where they will continue to flower for many years.

Right: all lilies should be considered as temporary house-guests rather than plants for growing indoors. Although many species can be grown in pots and brought indoors to flower, and indeed appreciate some protection from direct sunlight when in flower, most of the year they are better suited for the frost-free greenhouse or cold frame. However, they are not difficult to grow and their floral display, though relatively short lived indoors, is well-worth the extra effort and time involved.

amount of water given. When the flower buds are visible, begin giving dilute liquid nutrients. Repeat the feeds once every two weeks until the plants are in flower. Stop giving liquid fertilizer at this time, but continue watering. Once the flowers have faded, take the pots outdoors and let the plants die back naturally. Although the amount of water needed during the dormant season is relatively small, make sure the bulbs never dry out completely.

Lilies can be propagated by a variety of methods. Perhaps the easiest is division of overcrowded bulbs or roots, in the case of rhizomatous varieties, in the dormant season. Make sure the stock is virus-free, however, as viral infections are transmitted to new plants in vegetative propagation. Alternatively, new plants can be had from seed sown in autumn or from bulbils which are produced in the leaf axils.

Nerine

These South African bulbous plants produce packed umbels of deep red, pink or white trumpet-shaped flowers. Carried on stems 30-60cm (1-2ft) high they will add a touch of the exotic to a sunny room. Maximum light is essential and the plants do best when sited on shelves near the glass in the greenhouse, or in the lightest window indoors. They also need plenty of cool, fresh air, although the temperature should never drop below 10°C (50°F).

The three most commonly grown tender species are *Nerine flexuosa*, *Nerine sarniensis*, commonly called the Guernsey lily, and *Nerine undulata*; all are autumn flowering and all require similar cultivation. Plant the bulbs close together and shallowly in 15cm (6in) pots filled with a slightly heavy, well-drained potting mixture; shallow pans are better than full depth pots. Keep the roots dry during the summer months and gradually begin watering as the flower spikes and leaves appear. Water regularly until the plants die back at the end of their growing season then withhold water until the flower spikes appear the following summer.

After three years or so, the bulbs should be lifted and repotted into fresh compost. Remove the tiny offsets produced at the bases of the bulbs at this time and pot them up separately. New plants can also be had from seed, but this is a slow process, and the named cultivars will not come true if propagated in this way.

Vallota speciosa

The Scarborough lily has rich red, trumpet-shaped flowers carried on stems 45cm (18in) high and strap-shaped evergreen leaves. It is a most attractive late-summer flowering plant. Plenty of light is needed for them to thrive and they do best up against the glass in a greenhouse or on a light, airy windowsill indoors.

Plant the bulbs in 15cm (6in) pots in late summer in a reasonably heavy but well-drained potting mixture with the tops of the bulbs just visible above the surface of the compost. Keep the compost dry in summer and water moderately in winter, with generous amounts of water being given in spring. During the growing season, give regular applications of dilute liquid fertilizer, but it is best to keep the plants somewhat pot-bound.

Propagation is most simply done by removing the offsets found at the base of mature bulbs; do this in summer and pot the tiny bulbs in 7.5cm (3in) pots, repotting them as they grow.

Veltheimia viridifolia
These decorative South African indoor plants flower during the winter, a time of year when most plants are not at their best. The tubular flowers are very subtly coloured, basically pink with pale yellow, orange and green specking; they are pendulous and appear in a cluster on the tips of the stems, which are 45cm (18in) high. The leaves are broad and glossy green, and are an additional attraction.

Pot the bulbs in late summer or early autumn in a well-drained compost containing plenty of sand and a little bonemeal. The tips of the bulbs should just be showing above the surface of the compost. Keep moist while the plants are growing and flowering and feed regularly with dilute liquid manure. When the foliage has died down after flowering, the bulbs should be allowed to dry off and have a dormancy period before being started into growth the following autumn.

New plants can be had by separating clumps of older bulbs and potting up the young bulbs separately.

Right: Veltheimia viridifolia is a member of the lily family; its common name, unicorn root, refers to the pointed shape of the bulb. Quite tolerant of low temperature, it can be grown in a cool conservatory or greenhouse, as long as the temperature does not fall below 4°C (40°F).
Opposite: Vallota speciosa, or Scarborough lily, is a South African bulbous plant related to hippeatrum. It makes a fine, long-lasting display in late summer and has modest cultural requirements.

FOLIAGE PLANTS

When confronted with a display of indoor plants, most beginners will head straight for the flowering varieties. However, the more dependent a plant is on its flowers for beauty, and flowering constitutes only a short part of a plant's life cycle, the less likely it is that the leaf colour will be equally attractive.

Foliage plants, though perhaps not as glamorous at first sight, are much less ephemeral; their attractiveness is inherent and lasts virtually as long as the plant does. The intense colouring of a coleus leaf, for example, can equal that of any flower and theoretically can remain attractive for several years.

Although it takes a certain amount of sophistication to forgo the transient beauty of a flowering plant for the more subtle attractions of a highly coloured foliage plant, the most experienced growers eventually turn to foliage plants. Enthusiastic amateurs often ignore green as a colour, perhaps because most of the natural foliage in temperate zones is green and something more exciting or exotic is sought after. In fact, the range of greens and variegations based on green is enormous and the general effect is one of restfulness to the eye. Even the humble spider plant, with its fresh green and white foliage, comes into its own as a peaceful contrast to the frenzied colours of crotons. Ivy fanatics can marvel over the slightest subtle variation on the green and white theme, with new named forms being marketed every year. In fact many foliage plants, such as scheffleras, described as mid-green in colour, have elegant leaf shapes or habits of growth which can be better appreciated because of their cool, unhectic colour.

Acorus gramineus variegatus
A dainty, water-loving grass-like plant, acorus rarely grows taller than 25cm (10in). The green and white striped leaves grow in tufts and the plant is equally suitable for the edge of a pool outdoors or a pot filled with ordinary loam and placed in a shallow dish of water indoors. Acorus spreads by means of underground rhizomes and can be easily propagated by division.

Aechmea
This genus contains many attractive house and greenhouse plants. In their native habitats in Central and South America, they are found growing on the branches and trunks of trees and their star-shaped rosettes of leaves funnel rain water and plant debris to the base of the plant. Grow in indirect sunlight in a minimum temperature of 16°C (60°F). Never allow the plant to dry out and water directly into the central rosette; on hot dry days the plant should be sprayed with a mist of tepid water. The potting compost should be equal parts of loam, leafmould, peat and sand. Propagate by removing the young rosettes which form at the base of the parent plant with a sharp knife and repot in good soil.

Aglaonema
There are a number of handsome plants among the aglaonemas, all with white and green foliage and varying in height from 30-120cm (1-4ft). The most popular aglaonem is sold under the name of *A. crispum* 'Silver Queen'. Grow in moist, shaded conditions as a dry atmosphere tends to cause the leaves to shrivel and direct sunlight leads to scorching. The potting mixture should be equal parts loam and leafmould, with a sprinkling of sharp sand for drainage. Keep nearly dry during the dormant season and give plenty of water while it is growing. Propagate by division.

Ananas comosus variegatus
The pineapple plant rarely produces fruit when grown in temperate climates but the rosette of leaves, which are clear green with creamy-yellow margins, is very attractive and may grow to a height of 1m (3ft). Use a free-draining, loam-based compost

with manure and a little bonemeal added. Full sun is necessary and a moist atmosphere in spring and summer. Propagate from suckers which form at the base of the plant. Alternatively, use the top of an ordinary pineapple, leaving about 2.5cm (1in) of the crown attached. Allow it to dry for a couple of days, to prevent rotting, and insert the crown in a sandy compost. Keep warm until it has rooted.

Araucaria excelsa
The Norfolk Island Pine is an evergreen conifer which reaches a height of over 40m (130ft) in its native Australia, but when grown as a pot plant it rarely exceeds 1m (3ft). The slightly pendulous branches grow at right angles to the stem, creating a cedar-like effect, and are covered with masses of tightly packed, bright green needles. An airy sunny position is best for these plants. Pot in a loam-based compost with plenty of leaf mould and sharp sand added. Plants will need regular potting on in their first few years; never allow them to become root-bound. A minimum temperature of 7°C (45°F) is needed during winter and 12°-15°C (55°-60°F) in the growing season. To propagate, take cuttings from young shoots in autumn; keep the cuttings in a warm propagator until roots have formed.

Aspidistra elatior
The ability to survive harsh environments and near-total neglect make the cast iron plant, or parlour palm, as it is sometimes called, one of the most fool-proof indoor subjects. The glossy, spear-shaped green leaves are 60cm (2ft) tall and there is a pretty, variegated form with white-striped leaves; the flowers are inconspicuous. Grow in a well-drained, compost-based soil and give a minimum temperature of 10°C (50°F). Water freely in summer and moderately the rest of the year. A lightly shaded position is best; although heavy shade will not kill the plant, it should be avoided. Increase by division in spring.

Begonia
This genus contains hundreds of species of attractive perennial plants grown both for their foliage and

Above: Many varieties of begonia are cultivated solely for their wide range of coloured foliage.
Opposite: Hardy stalwart of the Victorian era, the aspidistra is able to withstand very harsh treatment, hence its common name, the cast iron plant.

their flowers. Generally, those grown as foliage plants are either fibrous rooted or rhizomatous; those grown for their flowers are tuberous-rooted and are listed under 'Flowering plants'. Varying in height from 7.5cm (3in) to over 1.5m (5ft), perhaps the most popular among the foliage begonias is *B. rex*. The asymmetrical, ovoid leaves are up to 30cm (1ft) long, and range in colour from metallic green through pink, deep red, dark purple, brown and silver. The Iron Cross begonia, *B. masoniana*, is so called because its pale green leaves are marked with a single brown cross in the centres. Foliage begonias should be grown in a mixture of loam, leafmould and well-rotted manure, with a sprinkling of sharp sand added. A light position, but shaded from direct sunlight, is desirable. Plants should be watered freely in summer and moderately the rest of the year. Always allow the soil to dry out a little before rewatering. Spray the foliage with tepid water during very hot weather.

Bilbergia nutans

This is one of the more modest bromeliads, yet is much loved and has become a favourite cottage plant. What it lacks in splendour, it makes up for in ease of cultivation. It is a quick-growing plant and is easily propagated by splitting up the clumps of glossy, dark green leaves once they have become crowded. Its small but enchanting flowers, which hang down from the top of an arching, stalk-like bract, are tubular and pink with unusual blue and green tips. Bilbergia's common name, angel's tears or queen's tears, comes from these pendulous flowers. Unfortunately, they only last for about a week, which is probably why they are not often available commercially. Give full sun, keep the temperature on the warm side and the plant well watered.

Calathea

This is quite definitely a difficult plant to manage, but it is among the most striking of all foliage plants and, if you can provide the right growing conditions, well worth attempting. From tropical South America, all calatheas require a minimum temperature of 18°C (65°F) and moist, shaded conditions. Although sold as houseplants, this is somewhat misleading as they really need a greenhouse to do well. During summer, the temperature should be at least 25°C (77°F) and the plants should be sprayed daily with tepid water and the compost kept moist. Use a rich but free-draining potting mixture and feed with weak liquid fertilizer when new leaves are being produced. To keep the atmosphere around the plant humid, put the pot inside a large container filled with moist peat or a shallow dish filled with pebbles and water.

There are well over one hundred species, the most attractive of which is *Calathea makoyana*, commonly called the peacock plant. When well grown, it can reach up to 1m (3ft) or more in height. The enormous oval leaves are silvery green with mid-green edges and central markings on either side of the mid-rib. The undersides are tinged with maroon. *Calathea ornata* is smaller growing, generally less than 60cm (2ft) high. The young leaves have thin pink stripes along the veins and the colour gradually changes to creamy white as the leaf matures. *Calathea zebrina*, the zebra plant, is a similar size, but the leaves have horizontal stripes of bright and dark green.

Propagation is by division of the rhizomes of mature plants in late spring or early summer.

Ceropegia woodii

This lovely, trailing plant gets its common name, hearts entangled, from the heart-shaped, succulent leaves on slender stems which twine around one another. These stems can be up to 1m (3ft) long, and the plant is best displayed in a hanging basket. Compared to many other trailing plants, the leaves of hearts entangled are rather sparse and large areas of the wiry stems are bare. The leaves are fleshy and marbled, greyish-green. Small white and purple, tubular flowers appear in summer, but these are relatively inconspicuous.

Hearts entangled is a South African plant and needs plenty of sun and reasonable warmth all year round. Use an ordinary, well-drained potting com-

post and avoid over-watering. Keep the compost practically dry during winter; water moderately the rest of the year. New plants are easily made by laying strands of growth on the surface of a box filled with peat; they will quickly root of their own accord and can then be severed from the parent plant and potted up individually.

Chlorophytum comosum

Agreeably easy to manage in almost any conditions, chlorophytum, or the spider plant, is an excellent subject for beginners, or even children, to grow, as it will tolerate considerable neglect and yet still manage to survive. It grows well in a wide range of temperatures and prefers good light, thorough watering and frequent feeding in the growing season. Plants suffering from shortage of nutrients will turn brown on the tips of the leaves. They should be potted on frequently, as they grow quickly and will suffer if they become pot-bound. Use a rich, reasonably heavy potting mixture.

Although the green and white variegated, grass-like leaves are not unattractive, the main charm of this plant lies in its method of reproduction. Perfectly shaped young plantlets develop on the stiff, arching stolons which radiate from the parent plant. These plantlets are simply pegged down in small pots filled with ordinary compost. Once they have rooted they can be severed from the parent plant. These hanging stolons mean chlorophytums are excellent subjects for hanging baskets or window boxes during the summer months. Although they will tolerate lower temperatures than many other indoor plants, they are not reliably frost hardy and should be taken indoors once cold weather sets in.

Cissus antarctica

Cissus antarctica, or Kangaroo vine as it is commonly called, is probably the most popular form of a large and varied genus of tropical plants which can be grown indoors. *Cissus antarctica*, in fact, is more useful than beautiful. Climbing to a height of 1.8m (6ft), the woody stems are densely clothed with broad, fresh green leaves with deeply toothed margins. It clings by means of tendrils and needs some form of support, preferably a trellis or net. Grown in a greenhouse border, it will rapidly cover large areas. The kangaroo vine needs an even temperature in the region of 15°C (60°F) to do well. However, temperatures can be slightly lower in the winter, provided the plant is kept fairly dry. Water generously and feed regularly during the growing season and protect from strong sunlight in the summer months. If it gets too hot or the atmosphere gets too dry, leaf-drop may result.

Propagation is by means of cuttings, about 10cm (4in) long, taken in summer and inserted into a peaty compost. Keep in a heated propagator until the cuttings have rooted, then pot them on. Easier, but slower and riskier, is to simply put the cuttings in jars filled with water and pot them up once roots have formed.

Citrus mitis

Although the small fruits of the Calemondin orange make first-class marmalade and thus the plant could be considered as a food crop, it is really for its decorative quality that it is grown. The bush rarely grows above 60cm (2ft) in height, but produces frag-

Cissus antarctica, or kangaroo vine, is a quick-growing vine and may need occasional pruning to keep it bushy.

rant white flowers while it is still young. It flowers right through the year, and if conditions are suitable the flowers are followed by small oranges, about 2.5cm (1in) in diameter.

Greenhouse conditions are ideal. If grown in the house, select the sunniest possible position in a room with a temperature that never falls below 10°C (50°F). When temperatures are cool, it is advisable to keep the root ball a little on the dry side. During the summer months, place them outdoors in full sun. This will help the new growth to ripen and thus ensure a good supply of flowers the next year. Keep the plants well watered during the summer months, and feed little and often with a dilute liquid fertilizer. In hot weather spray the foliage with tepid water regularly to keep the leaves from flagging.

New plants can be raised from 10cm (4in) long cuttings taken in spring and inserted in a peat and sand mixture in a heated propagator. Once the cuttings have rooted, pot them up into a rich, well-drained compost.

Codieaum variegatum pictum

This plant is better known by its common names, croton or Joseph's coat, the latter of which gives some indication of the intensity and variety of leaf colour. These are not easy plants to care for, and although tempting when seen in the shops in perfect condition, the beginner is advised to keep well away. They tend to drop their leaves if not given perfect conditions and can tax the ability of even the most green-fingered of growers. If, on the other hand, you cannot resist the temptation, or have been given one as a gift, then place it in the sunniest possible window. Make sure the temperature does not fall below 18°C (65°F) and avoid sudden temperature changes and exposures to draughts. Use a rich, well-drained potting compost and water and feed copiously in the growing season. Spray frequently with tepid water to keep the atmosphere moist and to discourage red spider mites, which are particularly attracted to crotons. In winter, water moderately; the leaves will be less colourful during the winter months, but quickly regain their brilliance with the increased light intensity in spring.

When grown as a houseplant, it is unlikely that they will exceed 60cm (2ft) in height. In greenhouses, which offer more suitable environments, they may reach a height of 1.5m (5ft) or more. The leaves, which are usually oval in shape, can be green, red, orange, yellow or deep brown, in colour, usually spotted, blotched or lined with contrasting colours.

Ten centimetre (4in) cuttings taken from the top of the plant will root if placed in a peat and sand mixture and kept at a temperature of 18°C (65°F) until rooting has occurred, then pot them up into a compost rich in nutrients.

Coleus blumei

The enormous range of colours and colour combinations of coleus foliage almost defies description. This tropical, evergreen perennial is easily grown from seed sown in spring and a single packet of mixed seeds can produce very impressive results. Unless you have room for masses of coleus, you should select the best of the young plants once the true

colours begin to show and either dispose of or give away the rest. Colours range from white, through yellow, orange, red, crimson, copper, maroon, purple, bronze, brown and green. There are many named forms with particularly striking patterns.

Although perennials in their native Java, in cultivation they are usually treated as annuals, with replacement plants grown yearly from seed or cuttings. They were favourite Victorian bedding-out plants, and are still often seen in public parks during the summer months. Indoors, give them a sunny window, moderate termperatures and plenty of water in spring and summer. They are quick-growers and reach a height of about 45cm (18in). To encourage bushy growth, pinch out the growing tips while the plants are young. The same goes for the inconspicuous flowers, which should be removed as soon as they appear. Use a rich, well-drained potting mixture and feed regularly during the growing season. In winter, when the amount of light available diminishes the leaves may look a little faded, but they will quickly pick up in spring. During the dormant season, keep the roots on the dry side and do not feed.

Cryptanthus

These are dwarf members of the bromeliad family and although lacking in the flamboyance of some of its larger relations, these perfectly shaped earth stars, or starfish bromeliads are perfect for dish and bottle gardens. They are relatively easy to care for, provided warmth and good light are given. As with other bromeliads, plenty of water in the growing season is needed, and just enough to keep the compost from drying out in the dormant season.

Cryptanthus bromeliodes 'Tricolor' is a gem of a plant with cream, pink, white and green leaves. This is one of the larger cryptanthus, and may reach a height and spread of 30cm (1ft). Much smaller, about 7.5cm (3in) in height and spread, are C.acaulis, C.bivittatus, C.fosterianus and C.zonatus. The leaves of all of these are highly coloured in various shades and combinations of white, pink, red, purple, green grey and brown. Many named forms are available.

Dieffenbachia

To start with a word of warning, all the plants in this genus contain a poisonous sap that can be particularly unpleasant should it get into the mouth or eyes, so keep them well out of the reach of children and pets. If the tongue comes into contact with the sap it will swell up, hence dieffenbachia's common name, dumb cane.

All this having been said, dieffenbachias are among the most attractive of exotic foliage plants and well worth growing if you can meet their exacting demands. Some of the more difficult species are really only suitable for greenhouse cultivation, but *Dieffenbachia picta* can be grown successfully indoors if the temperature never falls below 18°C (65°F). The species has cream and dark-green speckled colouring. However, there are named varieties available, such as *D.p.* 'Exotica', with glowing, pale-yellow leaves, and *D.p.* 'Bausei', with two-tone green leaves overlaid with silver spots.

Select a slightly shaded spot indoors and use a rich, peaty potting compost. To get the necessary humidity, plunge the pot into a larger container filled with moist peat and syringe the leaves in hot weather. Dieffenbachias are particularly vulnerable to draughts, so keep them well away from draughty positions. Most dieffenbachias tend to become a bit leggy with age and drop many of their lower leaves. *D.p.* 'Exotica' is better in this respect. It produces new plants from the base of the parent stem. These can be carefully cut away, with a little root attached, and potted up into a peaty mixture until fully established.

Dieffenbachia picta is an attractive but relately demanding plant which needs a warm environment to thrive.

Dracaena

This genus contains plants with a wide range of colours, shapes and habits. Most are tree-like in their growth and eventually form very stately plants. One of the few that remain reasonably compact is *Dracaena godseffiana* 'Florida Beauty'. This wide-branching shrub is painfully slow growing, but will eventually reach a height of 60cm (2ft). The dark-green and golden-yellow leaves are laurel-like and grow in sparse groups of two or three along the

Dracaenas make stately and elegant specimen plants in time; most species have a tree-like habit of growth.

branches. The best effect is achieved by grouping several young plants in a shallow pan so there is a good show of foliage and the same time ample space for the roots to grow.

Of the taller-growing species, much the easiest to manage is *Dracaena marginata*. It sheds its lower leaves as it increases in height and may eventually

92

look like a curious, spindly tree. 'Marginata' refers to the burgundy-coloured thin margin on the otherwise green leaf. It is more tolerant of low temperatures than other members of this genus and will over-winter in a cool room as long as it is frost free. Ideally, however, a temperature of around 15°C (60°F) is best.

Despite their relative costliness, there is always a demand for dracaenas and commercial growers have responded by continually introducing new named forms. Many of these are derived from *D.deremensis*, which has attractive green, grey and white markings and grows to a height of 1.2m (4ft) or more in a house; in a heated greenhouse it may double this height. Tropical in origin, it prefers temperatures in the region of 18°C (65°F), but needs a light and airy atmosphere and not the excessively humid conditions associated with forest-dwelling tropical plants. All dracaenas should have their roots kept on the dry side, particularly in winter. Use a rich, heavy potting compost rather than peaty one and feeding should begin only when the pots are well filled with roots.

Taller-growing dracaenas are not easily propagated by the amateur, but once the main plant becomes bare and leggy, you can try cutting the stem up into 10cm (4in) long sections and laying them on their sides in a seed box filled with peat and sand and kept at a temperature of 21°C (70°F). The mother plant will probably send up new growth and its appearance will be much improved. Once the stem cuttings have rooted and are sending out new leaves, pot them on individually into a richer compost.

Dracaena terminalis, one of the most popular and colourful of the straight-stemmed dracaenas, is now often listed as *Cordyline terminalis*. Whatever its name, its cultivation is similar to that for dracaenas, except that it will need more frequent watering, preferably with lime-free water. Its leaves are an unusually vivid red and it is produced in vast quantities on the European continent. Named forms have been developed with attractive red, pink or white variegated striped leaves.

Episcia cupreata

This compact tropical perennial can be grown as a trailing or creeping plant and, if carefully pruned, it will produce mounds of luxuriant foliage. The large, oval leaves are wrinkled and have a red and silvery-white stripe down the middle. Although it is primarily grown for the foliage, the small red tubular flowers are an additional bonus.

Warm, shaded conditions are necessary with temperatures not falling below 15°C (60°F). A particularly free-draining compost should be used with either plenty of peat and sharp sand or, alter-natively, grow in a compost which contains a high proportion of sphagnum moss. Keep the compost moist at all times and feed with weak liquid ferti-lizer during the growing season. Older plants may get slightly leggy. If so, replace them by allowing trailing pieces to root into a pot filled with peat and then sever the rooted plantlet from the parent plant.

Fatsia japonica

This slightly tender evergreen shrub is often seen growing outdoors, where in time it may reach a height of 3m (10ft) or more. When confined to a pot indoors, however, it is unusual to see one taller than 1m (3ft). Its large, glossy palmate leaves make quite a display and it seems to thrive on minimal care. There is a particularly beautiful variegated form with thin white margins on the leaves. Commonly called the Japanese aralia, false castor oil plant, or the figleaf palm, cool conditions and plenty of indirect light are necessary. Centrally heated rooms are not really suitable.

Use a reasonably rich, but free-draining loam, with plenty of sharp sand added. Water moderately during autumn and winter and regularly during the growing season. Propagation is from seed sown in spring or by removing suckers from the base of the plant and treating them as cuttings.

An interesting cross between *Fatsia* and *Hedera*, or ivy is × *Fatshedera lizei*. The leaves are very similar to those of fatsias, but its habit of growth is tall and spindly and it really needs to be given some form of support. Unlike ivy, it does not cling, so wire or plastic ties will be needed. Cultivation is the same as for fatsia.

Ficus

In this enormous and very varied genus are found a large number of popular indoor plants, each with slightly different cultivation requirements. There are a few general rules which apply to most of those commonly grown as houseplants. Keep the compost on the heavy side and use much less peat than nor-mally goes into a potting compost. Secondly, because the soil is heavy, avoid compressing it too much when potting up the plants or it will be compacted into a solid, airless lump. Most of the decorative figs will require potting on into slightly larger containers every other year while they are still growing. Once they are in 30cm (1ft) pots, keep them in good health by regular feeding.

The most popular species is *Ficus robusta*, the rubber plant. This is a considerable improvement on and has almost completely replaced the now seldom seen *Ficus elastica*.

The rubber plant needs relatively cool conditions

to thrive. Temperatures should be in the region of 13°C (55°F). Avoid over-watering and let the compost dry out a little from one watering to the next. Very wet conditions almost inevitably lead to a yellowing and loss of leaves.

Good light is needed for all ornamental figs, with the one possible exception of *Ficus pumila*, the creeping fig. Its small, fresh-green foliage is most attractive and it is ideal for hanging baskets or bottle gardens, but it needs shade and relatively moist growing conditions. If it is allowed to become very dry, the leaves, which are thin and delicate, will shrivel up and it is unlikely the plant will ever recover. The simplest means of propagation is to allow the creeping strands to root in pots filled with moist peat. Once they have rooted, sever them from the parent plant and pot up in to a richer compost.

Tall and stately, *Ficus benjamina*, commonly called the weeping fig, is a most handsome plant when well grown. If given insufficient light, it will slowly shed its leaves and can look fairly desolate. It also needs slightly higher temperatures to thrive; a minimum of 18°C (65°F) is best. Tip cuttings, about 7.5cm (3in) in length, can be taken at almost any time, if a heated propagator is available, but they will be slow in becoming established.

There are many other ornamental figs that will do well in conditions similar to those for the weeping fig. *Ficus lyrata*, the fiddle-leaf fig, is a superb large-growing plant if you want a bold effect. The huge, green leaves have prominent veins and resemble the body of a violin in shape. This species does make a sizable plant but it can be pruned back drastically during the winter months to keep it tidy. Perhaps a better solution is to re-site it where it can continue to grow.

There are a number of variegated forms of decorative fig, but few of them seem to do well as they all have the same tendency to produce leaves which develop brown patches along their margins.

Fittonia

Growing fittonias successfully is largely dependent on maintaining a sufficiently warm environment. A minimum of 18°C (65°F) is necessary and temperatures can go well above this with no ill effects. In recent years, the miniature form of *Fittonia argyroneura*, or snakeskin plant, as it is commonly called, has become fantastically popular. Its oval, deep-green leaves are heavily veined in silver and its compact habit of growth makes it ideal for bottle gardens or terrariums. It is extremely sensitive to lack of water. If conditions are too dry it will begin to collapse, but given water quickly enough it will recover without any permanent damage. In warm conditions cuttings will root with little difficulty.

Fittonia verschaffeltii is slightly more difficult to grow than *F.argyroneura*, as it really needs a heated terrarium. Both fittonias are similar in appearance, but *F. verschaffeltii* has slightly larger leaves which are heavily veined in carmine red. Fittonias need a rich, peaty growing mixture and because of their habit of growth they look better in shallow pots rather than full-depth containers.

Grevillea robusta

Tall, elegant and easy to care for, the silk oak is an evergreen shrub with delicate, feathery foliage. It is easily grown from seed and is relatively fast to develop; specimens in pots may reach 1.8m(6ft) in height, although 3m(10ft) is not unknown. Silk oaks which are not really oaks at all, are sometimes seen outdoors in summer-bedding schemes and in exceptionally sheltered, mild areas they can be grown as permanent planting. Indoors, they are best sited in a cool, semi-shaded spot. During the winter months they can be moved to a slightly sunnier position, but avoid exposure to full sun in hot summer weather. Use a rich, heavy potting mixture. Give plenty of water in spring and summer but while the plant is dormant give just enough water to keep the compost from drying out completely.

Gynura

There are two species of this handsome, tropical plant commonly available. *Gynura aurantica* and *Gynura sarmentosa* are somewhat similar in appearance, but the latter is a much more delicate and desirable subject. The long, pointed leaves are rich green and heavily veined and both the leaves and the stems are covered with fine, velvety purple hairs. It has a trailing habit of growth which makes it ideal for hanging baskets. Alternatively, provide some form of support against which to train the plant. Orange, daisy-like flowers appear in spring, but these have a most unpleasant scent and should be pinched out as soon as the buds are seen.

This practice will also help to keep the plant compact, as gynuras tend to get slightly leggy with age. Young plants are most attractive, as the older ones seem to lose much of their purple colour and gradually become quite dull. Ideally, they should be replaced every second year; cuttings taken in early spring root easily in a warm propagator and can be potted up once roots have formed.

Gynuras need shade during the summer months, but as much light as possible during winter. Keep the temperature moderately warm; 15°C(60°F) or thereabouts will suffice. Water sparingly in winter and freely the rest of the year. As the leaves are covered in fine hairs, avoid getting water on them or they will rapidly become discoloured and rot may set in. Use any ordinary potting compost with a little peat added to ensure free drainage.

Hedera

One of the best of all houseplants is *Hedera canariensis* or Canary Island ivy. It is ironic that it often is relegated to the garden outdoors after a mediocre performance inside. Outdoors, it flourishes and will quickly cover walls and fences with its glossy green and milky-white foliage. This gives an indication of the type of environment needed for ivy to do well as an indoor plant. Cool, light conditions are absolutely essential; a temperature of around 10°C(50°F) is ideal. In warm, centrally heated rooms ivy tends to dehydrate and also becomes very

Opposite: Ficus lyrata, the fiddle-leaf fig, is an exceptionally attractive foliage plant from tropical Africa. The large, wavy-edged leaves should have their upper surfaces cleaned regularly with a damp cloth.
Left: Fittonia argyroneura is South American in origin and requires warmth, humidity and shade to survive. Although it does not normally flower in cultivation, occasionally small, creamy yellow flowers are produced; these should be pinched out.

95

susceptible to infestation by red spider mite. In either case the plant will drop its leaves, whereupon it should be banished to the garden where the problem will correct itself naturally.

There are endless named forms available, with a wide variety of leaf shape, size and colour. Variegations range from bright, deep yellow, as in *Hedera helix* 'Gold Heart', through pale cream, white and yellow-green as in *H. colchica*, Paddy's pride. Variegated ivies can have leaves splashed with a central, contrasting colour or edged with another colour, or as in *H.h.* 'Marmorata', marbled and mottled with several colours. Leaf sizes range from very small, as in *H. helix* 'Cavendishii' and *H.h.* 'Chicago' to very large indeed. *H. colchica* 'Dentata variegata' is almost tropical in its luxuriant appearance. Its enormous leaves are bright green, variegated grey and pale cream in colour. As there are an enormous number of different forms available, ivies are perfect subjects for enthusiastic collectors and many an extensive collection has been built up over the years from odd cuttings.

Cuttings root quite easily when placed in a mixture of peat and sand. Place several cuttings around the edge of the pot and place the pot in a propagating case or plastic bag to reduce transpiration. Once the cuttings have rooted, pot them up in a peaty mixture. At regular intervals pinch out the growing tip to encourage side branches to form. Vigorous plants can be potted on annually in spring and all indoor ivies benefit from a spell outdoors in summer in a sheltered spot.

Helxine soleirolii
Mind-your-own-business, or baby's tears, as it is sometimes called, is a pretty little plant which makes mounds of tiny, fresh-green leaves. The form 'Argentea' has silver-variegated leaves, and *H.s.* 'Aurea' has bright, intensely yellow leaves. It will thrive in a cool temperature, as long as it is not subjected to frost. In very sheltered gardens helxine is sometimes grown outdoors, where it makes a neat ground cover. Good light is necessary, although protection from strong sunlight should be given. Older plants can tend to look overgrown. If this occurs, either cut back hard to encourage bushiness or make new plants in spring by snipping off a few pieces and pressing them into a peaty mixture in small pots and place them in a heated propagator until the cuttings have rooted.

Hypoestes sanguinolenta
The main attraction of this otherwise quite ordinary houseplant is the pattern of small pale-pink dots which appear on the mid-green, heart-shaped leaves.

The lilac-coloured flowers in summer are quite insignificant and are usually pinched out to keep the plant bushy. A native of Madagascar, it grows to a height of about 60cm (2ft). The stems are wirey, however, and plants tend to become straggly and thin after a while. When this happens, prune back hard and new growth should appear shortly thereafter.

Hypoestes needs plenty of light, although protection from direct sunlight should be given. Water freely in the growing season, and keep the temperature above 18°C (64°F) at all times. Use any ordinary well-drained compost and propagate from seed or cuttings.

Kentia
This elegant palm is one of the most expensive houseplants and yet there is never a shortage of purchasers. Also called *Howea*, after Lord Howe Island in the Pacific Ocean where it grows, it is very tolerant of shade and makes a perfect indoor plant. There are two species of Kentia, *K. belmoreana* and *K. forsteriana* but they are virtually indistinguishable. There is no central trunk, but a number of leaf stems up to 1.8m (6ft) high. The fronds are divided into many arching leaflets, which spread out, giving a fan-like effect.

Young plants require potting on every other year. Use a compost containing peat and a liberal amount of rotting leaves — if a proprietary mixture is used, then add the other ingredients before potting.

Keep the plant in a good light but shade from strong sunlight; the temperature should never fall below 15°C (60°F). Keep the roots moist at all times and give an occasional spray with a mist spray during the summer. Scale insects on the stems and undersides of the leaves can be a nuisance but frequent misting will do much to eradicate this problem. However, chemical pesticides may be necessary to completely eradicate them. When cleaning the leaves use a damp cloth or sponge as chemical cleaners can be extremely damaging. If the leaf tips turn brown, it is probably because the drainage hole in the bottom of the pot has become blocked. The best remedy is to carefully knock the plant out of the pot and inspect and clear the hole. Propagation is by seed sown in early spring in a heated propagator. However, seed may be difficult to find.

Maranta
Despite its delicate appearance, marantas are tough evergreen perennial houseplants which can hold

Variegated ivies make durable, long-lived and long-suffering plants but appreciate a spell outdoors in summer.

their own given reasonable care. The leaves are oval, bright green and marked with deep maroon blotches between the lateral veins. *Maranta leuconeura* 'Erythrophylla', sometimes called the red herring-bone plant has pale crimson veins and midribs, and yellow-green stripes along the central veins. *Maranta leuconeura* 'Kerchoveana', or rabbit's tracks, has greyish green leaves spotted with red on both sides of the central veins. The leaves of Marantas close up at night, like hands folded in prayer; for this reason it is often referred to as the prayer plant.

Natives of tropical Brazil, these prostrate plants need protection from strong sunlight, a minimum temperature of 15°C (60°F) and plenty of moisture in spring and summer. In autumn and early winter, water moderately; thereafter, until spring, keep the compost nearly dry. Use a peaty free-draining mixture and feed regularly during the growing season. They are fairly greedy feeders and should be repotted annually. Marantas are rhizomatous plants, and can be easily propagated by dividing the rhizomes in mid-spring. Insert the pieces, each with two or three leaves attached, into pots filled with pure peat and put the pots in a heated propagator.

Monstera deliciosa

Very much a tropical jungle plant, Monstera has adapted to indoor cultivation and is now one of the most popular of all foliage houseplants. The Swiss cheese plant, as it is commonly called, has large glossy leaves with deeply cut serrations when mature; young leaves are heart-shaped and entire. Mature plants have creamy white arum-like flowers usually in summer. These are followed, in autumn by cylindrical fragrant fruit.

In its native Mexico, it grows as a climber, clinging by means of aerial roots which grow out from every node. In cultivation, it can become somewhat of an unruly creature and needs strong support. This involves tying in new growth as it develops, being careful to take into account the fact that the growth will swell and should have room to expand. The best support is a strong hardwood stake to which a thick layer of moist sphagnum moss has been attached with nylon fishing line. As the stout aerial roots appear from the main stem, train them in to the mossed support. Not only will this improve the appearance of the plant, but the roots will be able to draw moisture from the moss. Some plants will

Marantas, though seemingly quite delicate, will thrive and increase rapidly in size if given warmth, shade, and plenty of water in the growing season. They are sometimes called prayer plants because the leaves tend to fold up at night, like hands in prayer.

produce an almost unbelievable number of these roots and, although you can thin them out, most should remain. As the roots lengthen, they should be directed into the soil in the pot. Alternatively, place a container nearby filled with water and train the roots into this. The plant will then draw moisture directly from the container and subsequent growth will be much more vigorous. Also, much less water will be required in the pot filled with compost. When watering the pot, allow the soil to dry out a little between waterings. Dilute feeds of liquid fertilizer should be given little and often during the growing season, rather than occasional heavy doses. Wipe the leaves periodically to keep them shiny and free from dust but avoid handling the delicate new topmost leaves.

Young plants will require potting on into slightly larger containers every other year until they are in 30cm (12in) pots; thereafter, keep them in good order by regular feeding. The potting mixture should be rich and on the heavy side and any repotting or potting on is best done in spring.

It is possible to propagate monsteras by removing large sections from the top of the plant and potting them up into a peaty mixture. The section should contain two or three leaves and some aerial roots. It is a good idea to allow the severed end to dry out a little before inserting into the compost; keep the temperature high, a minimum of 24°C (75°F), until the cuttings have rooted.

Musa

Although seeds of banana plants are offered by some of the more spectacular seed catalogues and the occasional young plant may be for sale at a nursery or garden centre, think twice before buying one. Like the irresistible puppy in the pet store window, once you get it home the demands are probably more than you bargained for. Unless you have a very large greenhouse, and they do need greenhouse cultivation, the most suitable specie is *Musa velutina*, which rarely exceeds 1.5m (5ft) in height. Unfortunately, the fruit, which is an attractive red colour, is inedible. Slightly larger, reaching 1.8m (6ft) in height and spread is *Musa ensete*, but it does not fruit, or even flower in cultivation.

The plant needs plenty of room in which to develop; its large, spreading leaves may be more than 1m (3ft) long. It is often grown in the greenhouse border, or in large pots filled with rich, well-drained compost. A minimum temperature of 18°C (65°F) is needed and exposure to light but it should be shaded from full sunlight in the hottest summer weather. Water and feed generously through spring and summer, while new growth is being made. Give

no liquid fertilizer and water sparingly at other times.

Musa ensete can be propagated from seed sown in a heated propagator. *M. velutina* has a suckering habit of growth and new plants can be had by dividing the clumps in early spring. The stem which has produced the flowers will die after flowering and fruiting, and should be cut out. In any case, banana plants almost inevitably begin to deteriorate indoors once they reach full height, but by then may have given a certain amount of pleasure and fulfilled the grower's need for the unusual and exotic.

Neanthe bella

The parlour palm has a confusing number of names; it is sometimes listed as *Chamaedorea elegans* and occasionally as *Neanthe elegans* or *Collinia elegans*. Whatever its name, it is a delightful little plant and an extremely popular one. Mexican in origin, it has appearance of a typical palm, with hanging, bright green pinnate leaves, up to 1.2m (4ft) long growing on a stout ringed stem. The latter may, in time, attain a height of several metres, but it grows slowly and this possibility should not deter you from purchasing a small one; several years may elapse between each potting-on operation.

In nature these palms grow in the shade of taller plants and should never be exposed to full sunlight. Maintain a minimum temperature of 15°C (30°F) and give them a well-drained growing compost, with plenty of peat and sand. Water generously in spring and summer and moderately the rest of the year; propagation is from seeds.

Pandanus

The screw pine, as it is commonly called, is somewhat of a rarity as far as commercial growers are concerned and consequently rather difficult to find in the shops. It is, however, one of the most spectacular of foliage plants and well worth growing for its beautiful variegated leaves. Mature specimens of *Pandanus candelabrum* may reach a height of 2m (6ft) with a similar spread and not every house has room for one. There are smaller species available, such as *P. sanderi* and *P. veitchii*, which rarely grow more than 1m (3ft) high in cultivation. The leaves are broad, arching and bright green, with either gold, silvery or white stripes. Some varieties have sharp spines along the margins and undersides. The leaves grow from a central rosette and the mature leaves and trunks tend to develop a twist, hence its common name.

Tropical in origin, screw pines need warmth, moisture and plenty of light, although some protection from direct sunlight in summer may be necessary. Never let the temperature fall below 13°C

(55°F) and be careful not to overwater in winter, or the plant may rot. During the growing season, give plenty of water and spray regularly with a mist sprayer to create a humid atmosphere. Alternatively, put the pot in which it is growing into a larger container filled with moist peat or pebbles so that the evaporating water will create a moist atmosphere. The plants will benefit from feeding at regular intervals during the growing season with dilute liquid fertilizer; if they need potting on, do so in mid-spring. Propagation is by means of the offsets produced at the base of mature plants; detach them in spring and put up in a mixture of peat and sand.

Peperomia

There are masses of peperomias from which to choose and all are reasonably easy if given a well-lit position, a temperature of about 15°C (60°F) and moderate amounts of water. Almost all are compact plants which are ideal if space is limited and make excellent subjects for bottle gardens. Although there are more than 1,000 species and many of these are commercially available, one or two are almost universally popular. *Peperomia caperata* is one of these. It has deep green, fleshy leaves which are impressed along the veins, giving each leaf a sculptural appearance. Creamy white flower spikes appear above the foliage from spring through winter although the flowers themselves are insignificant. Another is *Peperomia hederaefolia*, a similar plant with slightly larger leaves which are smooth, rounded and steel grey in colour. *Peperomia magnoliaefolia* is a freely branching species with a loose habit of growth; its oval, fleshy leaves are produced on purple stems and *P.m. variegata* is a named form with particularly attractive cream and green variegations.

Philodendron

Many species of this genus are quite massive and totally unsuited for indoor culture, while others are almost indispensible as houseplants. With the increasing popularity of hydroponics, moisture-loving philodendrons would seem to have an assured future. Although there are variegated kinds and others with a reddish tinge to the foliage, most are

Right: Peperomia magnoliae-folia, one of the many species of this low-growing, succulent genus of foliage plants available. South and Central American in origin, peperomias are usually epiphytic in the wild; when grown as pot-plants they need relatively little soil compared to their above-ground growth. All species are easily propagated from cuttings taken in spring or summer and inserted in a mixture of sand and peat. The cuttings will root more quickly if bottom heat is given. Opposite: Philodendron 'Green Emerald'. South American in origin, philodendrons rarely flower in cultivation but are grown for their impressive foliage. The leaves are either entire or deeply incised, depending on the species, although some species have quite different juvenile and adult foliage.

glossy dark green. All have the same cultural requirements, however, and do well in conditions offering
light shade, moist root conditions and humidity;
plunging the plant's pot into a larger container filled
with moist peat or moss will help to provide the
humidity, as will regular spraying of the foliage with
tepid water. Temperatures in the region of 18°C
(65°F) are recommended although 14-16°C (57-60°F)
is acceptable during winter for all but the variegated
philodendrons, which need slightly warmer conditions. All require rich, free-draining, peaty composts.
New plants can be raised from cuttings taken in

summer or from seed, although the latter is not
easily obtained.

Philodendron scandens, or the sweetheart plant, has
heart-shaped, glossy green leaves and will climb or
trail, depending on whether or not it is provided with
a support. In America it is often called the bathroom
plant, probably because of its preference for the
warm, humid atmosphere so often found in bathrooms.

Philodendron tuxla, sometimes listed as *P.hastatum*
has much larger, spear-shaped leaves and develops
into a sizable plant even when confined to a pot,

4m (13ft) high is not unusual. It is advisable to provide a mossed support up which it can grow. Another large-leaved species is *P. bipinnatifidum*; erect-growing, the deeply incised leaves can be 60cm (2ft) long, and nearly as much across.

Phoenix

Although most of these palms eventually grow to enormous heights, they make very attractive pot-plants when young, their delicate, feathery fronds adding a touch of the exotic to a warm, sunny room. The smallest species available is *Phoenix roebelinii*, which is practically stemless and rarely grows taller than 1.8m (6ft). The deep green fronds are made up

of many leaflets. Each new frond is enclosed in a stiff spike which gradually unfolds, to reveal a ladder-like leaf covered in a fine, silvery powder. Although new fronds appear infrequently, they are most attractive when they do. Similar, but slightly coarser in appearance, is *Phoenix canariensis*. Both slowy develop into substantial plants, but *P. canariensis* is capable of reaching a height of 9m (30ft); grown in pots it never attains this height, although it can reach 4m (13ft) in suitable growing conditions. The light green fronds, which are composed of narrow, delicate leaflets, arch gracefully from a central trunk.

These palms need to be grown in good light and a moderately warm atmosphere, although winter temperatures can be quite low as long as they remain above freezing. Use a free-draining compost. Water well in spring and summer and sparingly the rest of the year. If, as is most unlikely, seed is available, new plants can be raised in this way. Seeds from the ordinary date can be sown in a sandy compost and in time will germinate into a tiny date palm, *P. dactylifera*.

Pilea

There are a number of these tropical, evergreen perennials available in the shops, all of which are neat and attractive when young but become straggly and untidy as they age. For this reason, they tend to be treated as short-term plants, but cuttings taken from mature specimens will root easily and can be used as replacements. The most popular is *P. cadierei*, commonly known as the aluminium plant because of the attractive, silvery-grey variegations on the oval, dark-green leaves. It grows to a height of 30cm (1ft) but the form *P.c.* 'Nana' is much more compact, reaching a height of 20cm (8in) and also less liable to become straggly in appearance. *Pilea muscosa*, sometimes listed as *Pilea microphylla*, is quite different in appearance. It has a bushy habit of growth and the leaves are tiny and silvery grey. The small, insignificant pale green flowers appear in spring and summer. When the flower buds come into contact with moisture, they burst open, discharging pollen from the anthers, hence its common names, 'artillery plant' or 'gunpowder plant'.

All pileas do well in warm conditions with shelter from direct sunlight. Keep them reasonably moist and feed during the growing season. The rest of the year reduce the amount of water given but never let

Left: Pittosporum tobira has glossy leaves and masses of sweetly-scented, tubular flowers in the summer months.
Opposite: a selection of pileas displayed en masse; they tend to get leggy but new plants are easily propagated.

the compost dry out completely. The general appearance of the plant will be vastly improved if you remove the growing tips regularly to encourage bushiness. Propagate from 10cm (4in) long cuttings taken in spring and insert into pots containing a peaty compost. Keep the pots in a heated propagator until the cuttings have rooted.

Pittosporum

Although mainly sold as garden plants for sheltered, mild areas, pittosporums also make good indoor plants if you can provide cool growing conditions; warm, dry centrally heated rooms are unsuitable. *Pittosporum undulatum* 'Variegatum' is an exceptionally beautiful plant, with shiny, large, wavy-edged leaves which are predominantly silvery-white. Pale, sweetly scented flowers are produced in late spring and early summer. Less striking, but probably more popular, is *Pittosporum tobira*, with its shiny, dark-green, oblong leaves which grow in whorls of five around the stems. It, too, has pale, sweetly-scented flowers in summer and can fill a whole room with an orange blossom-like fragrance.

Relatively slow growing, both plants may in time reach a height of 4 m(12ft) when grown in a large pot filled with a rich, heavy, but well drained compost. Give them plenty of light and air, and generous amounts of water during the growing season. If the plant gets straggly, prune it back hard after flowering. Propagate by taking cuttings with three or four leaves attached in spring and inserting them into a sandy rooting medium in a heated propagator.

Rhoicissus rhomboidea

One of the toughest of all indoor plants, grape ivy will grow in almost any situation. It is also one of the most popular indoor plants and there is scarcely an office or home without one. However, it is not really an ivy at all, but a member of the grape family. South African in origin, it climbs by means of curling tendrils which cling to supports. If grown in a greenhouse border, it can reach a height of 6m (20ft) or more. In a pot, however, it rarely exceeds 1.8m (6ft). The main attraction is the glossy evergreen foliage. Equally attractive is the speed with which it grows, as even modest care will lead to a rapid increase in the plant's size.

Grow in a rich, well-drained potting compost and give plenty of light, but protect from hot sunlight during summer. In fact, they will also grow quite happily in dimly lit corners, where many other plants would fail. Keep them well watered and fed during the growing season but during the dormant period keep them relatively dry. Grape ivy will tolerate

quite low temperatures in winter, as long as it is not exposed to frost. When the plants become dusty, stand them in the bath, and hose them down with tepid water. They are easily propagated from cuttings taken in mid spring.

Sansevieria

There are two species of Sansevieria in common cultivation, both requiring good light, temperatures in the region of 15°C (60°F) and miniscule amounts of water. *Sansevieria trifasciata*, or mother-in-law's tongue, is the taller of the two, growing to a height of 45cm (18in) or more, and the one most often seen. The variety 'Laurentii' has pale yellow margins on the leaves. *Sansevieria hahnii* is rather like a stumpy, compressed version of mother-in-law's tongue. It rarely grows taller than 15cm (6in) and is variegated dark green and pale grey in horizontal bands.

Sansevierias are very slow growing and potting on of established plants is only necessary if the plants break the pots in which they are growing; use a reasonably heavy compost. Water moderately in spring and summer, leaving long enough intervals between waterings for the compost to dry out completely. In winter they should be kept virtually dry. Cold, wet growing conditions can be fatal, so keep them warm and dry at all costs; the temperature should not really fall below 10°C (50°F). New plants can be had by carefully removing the young suckers which grow at the base of mature plants and potting them up in a reasonably rich compost.

Saxifraga sarmentosa

Also called *Saxifraga stolonifera*, its common name, 'mother-of-thousands' is a very descriptive one. The most intriguing aspect of this plant is its method of reproducing itself; young, perfectly formed plantlets are formed on the ends of long stolons which hang from the base of the mother plant. Even without this adornment, the plant is an attractive one. Growing to a height and spread of 30cm (12in), the leaves, which grow in loose rosettes, are slightly hairy, round and mid-green with a slightly reddish tone on the undersides. There is a named form, 'Tricolor' which has leaves splashed with pale cream and pink, but this is slightly more difficult to grow. Towards the end of summer, tiny white delicate flowers are produced in racemes on stiff stalks and they remain in flower over several weeks.

Although mother-of-thousands is not completely hardy, it is sometimes grown outdoors in sheltered, semi-shaded sites. Indoors, it needs fairly cool conditions, a reasonable amount of light and plenty of water during the growing season. It looks best when grown in a hanging basket, so the red stolons, which may be up to 60cm (2ft) long, can be fully displayed. Propagation is by pegging down the plantlets in pots of moist peat and severing the stolon once rooting has occurred.

Schefflera actinophylla

A mature, well-grown schefflera is one of the most impressive of indoor plants. An Australian, evergreen shrub, it will reach an eventual height of 1.8m (6ft) or more. The shining, pointed oval leaflets grow in groups of three or five at the end of leaf stalks which emanate from a central stem. The general effect is that of an elegant, tropical tree growing indoors.

Adequate temperature is essential, not less than 18°C (65°F) and plenty of indirect light. As the plants grow larger, they will need repotting every other year until they are in 30cm (1ft) pots, filled with a rich, peaty mixture. Water regularly right through the year and give them feeds of dilute liquid fertilizer in the growing season. Scheffleras are easily grown from seed sown in spring in a minimum temperature of 21°C (70°F).

Scindapsus aureus

There is a plethora of confusing names attached to this plant; sometimes called golden pothos, it is also referred to as *Raphidophera*, devil's ivy and money plant. Though ivy-like in its trailing habit of growth, it is in fact related to the philodendron family and not to the ivies at all. The pointed, oval, glossy leaves are streaked with yellow. The named variety 'Marble Queen' has white, green-flecked leaves and 'Tricolor' has leaves which are green, yellow and white.

Originally from the Solomon Islands, it needs a warm, moist atmosphere and protection from direct sunlight. Water generously from the beginning of the growing period in spring through autumn and moderately the rest of the year. The growing compost should be very free draining with plenty of peat and sphagnum moss. Although it is usually grown as a trailing plant, it can also be trained up sections of tree tunks or walls. Propagate by division of roots or from short stem cuttings. If a plant grows too large for the space allotted to it, prune back hard in late spring. The prunings can then be used to make more plants.

Senecio macroglossus

This is an attractive rampant climber, with glossy dark evergreen leaves; it is most often seen in its variegated form, *S.m.* 'Variegatus'. South African in origin, the common name, Cape ivy, refers to its ivy-like leaves and it produces large, rich-yellow, daisy-like flowers in winter. A light, sunny position

A young Scindapsus aureus, or golden pothos; eventually it makes a large, gracefully trailing specimen.

with a reasonable amount of warmth is necessary for it to thrive and plenty of water in the summer months. Unfortunately, Cape ivy is very vulnerable to greenfly, and a close watch must be kept against these pests. To maintain clean, healthy plants, new cuttings should be rooted and fresh plants grown on each year; these are easily grown in any open, peaty mixture.

Sparmannia africana

This plant has a number of common names, 'African windflower', 'African hemp' and 'indoor lime', each referring to some aspect of its character. If grown in the borders of a greenhouse it will eventually form a small tree. In pots it will still reach a good size, 1.2m (4ft) or so. The attractive, large, light-green leaves are covered on both sides with fine hairs and white flowers with yellow stamens appear in summer.

A rich, heavy, well-drained compost is best and plenty of water from mid-spring through mid-autumn. Keep the compost barely moist during the dormant season and, if necessary, prune hard in early winter. Cuttings of young shoots taken in spring should root fairly easily. Sparmannias can withstand cool temperatures in winter, as long as they are not subjected to frost; in summer stand them in a sunny sheltered site outdoors.

Tillandsia

These fascinating bromeliads are from tropical South America; most of those cultivated as pot-plants are epiphytic and do best when their roots are wrapped with sphagnum moss and attached to a small segment

out. They are easily propagated by detaching the small offshoots formed at the base of the rosette and potting them on individually.

Tolmeia menziesii

This coarse-leaved, evergreen foliage plant would probably not merit a second glance if it were not for its fascinating way of producing young plantlets in the centre of the parent leaf. This gives the plant its common name, the pick-a-back plant, and these young plants can be easily removed and potted up in a peaty mixture to grow on. This plant will also grow outdoors in a semi-shaded position so is ideal for the cool, airy room indoors. North American in origin, the foliage eventually reaches a height of 22cm (9in). Tall spikes appear in early summer which carry inconspicuous, bell-like flowers. Tolmeias need plenty of water when growing and flowering, but keep them nearly dry during the dormant season.

Tradescantia

Tradescantias depend on plenty of light to retain the colour in their foliage; if grown in dimly lit or shaded conditions, the attractive variegated or pink flushed leaves quickly turn pale and dull. It is basically for the foliage colour that these plants are grown, as the ovate or oblong leaves are not particularly interesting in shape and their pendulous habit of growth is slightly untidy, though eminently suitable for hanging baskets.

Tradescantia albiflora is the familiar wandering Jew which is a universally popular pot-plant. This is usually available as a variegated plant, either green and white or green, pink and white. *T. blossfeldiana* is slightly more erect in its habit of growth and its leaves are dark green underneath: it produces pink flowers over a long period in spring and summer.

Besides plenty of light, *Tradescantias* thrive in a temperature of 10-15°C (50-55°F). If the temperature falls below this, they tend to become thin and straggly. Although it could hardly be called an exciting plant, the ease with which it is propagated is its most noteworthy quality. Cuttings root almost instantaneously when inserted in ordinary potting compost; put several to a pot for the best effect. Once the cuttings have rooted the growing tips should be removed to encourage branching. Occasionally smaller sections will develop totally green

of a tree branch so that air can circulate freely around the leaves and roots. Alternatively, if grown in pots, a very free-draining, peaty mixture should be used, as waterlogging is fatal.

There are hundreds of species of tillandsia but most of the popular ones are rosette in form, with narrow, evergreen leaves radiating out from a central core. In the centre of the rosette is a curious flattened bract on which appear flowers of the most intense colouring. One of the best is *Tillandsia cyanea*, which has a bright pink, cuttlefish-shaped bract along which appear the blue flowers, either singly or two at a time. *T. lindeniana* is another good species; it is much larger than *T. cyanea* and reaches a height and spread of 50cm (20in). The dark blue and white flowers appear in summer on the curious pink inflorescence which is composed of overlapping bracts.

They prefer growing conditions similar to the tropical forests where they grow naturally, a temperature of not less than 18°C (65°F), filtered light, a moist atmosphere, and plenty of water during the growing season. When the plants are dormant, give just enough water to keep the compost from drying

instead of variegated; remove them immediately or the plant will quickly revert to dull green.

Vriesia splendens

This bromeliad gets its common name, flaming sword, from the tall, bright red spear-shaped bract which stands well away from the central urn. The flowers, which appear in late summer, are small, tubular and insignificant and it is really for its foliage and bract that it is grown. The leaves, which form a typical bromeliad rosette, are deep green, cross-banded with stripes of browny-black.

South American in origin, vriesias need quite a high temperature to do well; 21°C (70°F) is not excessive. Shade, a moist atmopshere and plenty of water in the growing season are necessary. Keep the plant relatively dry for the remainder of the year. Propagate by removing the young offsets formed at the base of the plant and let them dry out for a day or two before inserting them in a peaty compost.

Zebrina pendula

This trailing plant is closely related to the *Tradescantias* and indeed, its common name, wandering Jew is also used for one of the Tradescantias; the same cultivation applies to both. The attractive foliage is maroon on the reverse side and silvery and green on the upper surface.

FERNS

Ferns today are undergoing something of a revival in terms of their popularity as houseplants. During the Victorian era in Britain they were among the most popular of indoor subjects but, as fashions changed and a reaction against all things associated with the somewhat dour image of the Victorians set in, ferns slowly fell out of favour.

Today, however, they are once again being given the appreciation they deserve. Like all foliage plants, ferns have many advantages over flowering plants as indoor subjects. Perhaps the most important is that the majority are evergreen and are at their best virtually all-year-round, although one or two are deciduous and have a dormant season during which the above-ground growth disappears. In addition, they have one characteristic which makes them an almost ideal subjects for growing indoors. As most ferns grow in shady places in their natural environment, they are eminently suitable for growing in rooms with a low level of light; a dimly lit corner, that can mean instant death for a plant such as a cyclamen, can provide an ideal spot for a fern.

Botanically, ferns are living relics from a much earlier age and have changed little since they first developed, nearly 400 million years ago. What sets ferns apart from other plants is their curious and complicated method of reproduction. Ferns are non-flowering plants, and although they can be propagated from division or layering in cultivation, they reproduce themselves in nature by means of spores. These spores are produced on the underside of the fronds and can be seen as rows of tiny dark bumps. When they are ripe, the spores are released, rather like clouds of pollen, into the air. If they land on a suitable growing medium, each of these microscopic spores produces a prothallus. This tiny green growth is not a baby fern, in the way that a seed from a flowering plant produces a tiny new plant, but is really an intermediate stage in the development of a new fern, and it contains the male and female organs which are lacking in the mature, asexual fern. When the male cells from the prothallus have fertilized the female ones, the baby ferns develop and the cycle is completed.

Ferns range in height from 5cm(2in) to 20m(65ft) or more and in ease of cultivation from simple to virtually impossible; the latter are obviously best left to botanical gardens. All the ferns included here are readily available and well within the scope of the amateur indoor gardener.

Adiantum capillus-veneris
The maidenhair fern is perhaps the most delicate and beautiful of ferns, with its jet-black stalks and bright lacy foliage. Easily available from florists' shops, it is a very demanding subject and, more often than not, gradually deteriorates in health and vigour once it leaves the shop. It is worth the challenge, however, as a well grown maidenhair fern can be the focal point of a whole room or conservatory. Reaching a height and spread of 30cm(1ft) it is temperate in origin, and it will survive outdoors in a very sheltered and favourable site. A moist atmosphere and indirect light are essential if the plant is to thrive; it is also an excellent subject for Wardian cases or bottle gardens. A much tougher member of the same family is *Adiantum cuneatum*; similar in appearance to *A. capillus-veneris*, the fronds may reach a length of 37cm(15in).

Asparagus plumosus
Although not botanically ferns, these members of the lily family have the delicate graceful foliage and attractive habit so often associated with ferns. *Asparagus plumosus*, commonly called asparagus fern grows to a height of 3m(10ft) in its native South Africa. The cultivated form, however, is quite

compact and rarely reaches 60cm(2ft) in height. It is much loved by florists and flower arrangers and it is often included in bouquets of long-stemmed roses. When growing in the wild, it is a climber; should it show any tendency to climb indoors the tips of the developing shoots should be pinched off.

A member of the same family, *A. sprengeri*, sometimes called 'Emerald feather' because of its intense green colouring, has arching stems up to 1.2m (4ft) in length. It can be trained vertically up wires or canes, but looks best grown in a hanging basket, with the stems trailing down. Although primarily grown for their foliage, both types of asparagus fern produce inconspicuous white flowers, followed occasionally by attractive red berries.

Grow asparagus ferns in a well-lit position, but out of direct sunlight. Water and spray them freely during summer and give liquid fertilizer every two or three weeks while they are growing. Water

Adiantum capillus-veneris, or maidenhair fern, is an exquisite plant when well grown, but is a difficult subject.

moderately the rest of the year, but never allow the soil to dry out. A minimum winter temperature of 7°C(45°F) is essential and should the trailing stems of *A. sprengeri* grow too long, cut back hard to encourage new growth. A rich mixture of loam, leaf mould, peat and sharp sand for drainage is best and propagation is by division of the crowns in spring. Alternatively, sow the seeds in spring, with a minimum temperature of 21°C(70°F).

Asplenium bulbiferum

The common name of this plant, mother spleen-wort, is derived from the fact that tiny new ferns develop as bulbils along the fronds. In time, the bulbils will weigh the fonds down and new plants can easily be had by pegging them down in pans of moist compost. The finely divided deep-green fronds may reach a height and spread of 60cm(2ft). It is a good beginner's fern and thrives in cool

growing conditions, with protection from direct sunlight.

Asplenium nidus-avis

The spleenworts come in a variety of shapes and sizes, but the most commonly seen, and the most popular, is the bird's nest fern, *Asplenium nidus avis*. It is unlike most other ferns in appearance, as the bright green, spear-shaped fronds are entire, that is, the margins are smooth and not indented or perforated in any way. When well grown, the fronds can reach up to 1.2m (4ft) long. As they radiate from a central crown, the plant looks a little like a shuttlecock. In the wilds of tropical Asia, bird's nests ferns are found growing as epiphytes on tree limbs. In cultivation, they do best in full shade and plenty of warmth; a minimum of 18°C(65°F) is necessary. Use a rich, peaty mixture with plenty of coarse sand when potting up; water frequently in spring and summer and sparingly the rest of the year. Propagation is from spores in early spring or late summer, but this is a fairly difficult operation, and best left to the experts.

Athyrium goeringianum

The Japanese painted fern, with its delicate grey-green and silver fronds, is a tender relative of the hardy Lady fern, a native of England. It grows to a height and spread of 45cm(18in) and does best in a 15cm(6in) pot filled with a potting mixture made of loam, peat, leaf mould and sharp sand. A minimum winter temperature of 10°C(50°F) is needed and a draught-free position in indirect light. The Lady fern (*A. felix femina*) is sometimes collected from hedgerows and woodlands and potted up as an indoor plant, but it is deciduous and gives little pleasure in winter. Propagation is by spores, or division of crowns in April.

Cyrtomium falcatum

The holly-leaf fern is a native of Japan and rivals the aspidistra in its ability to withstand adverse growing conditions. Growing to a height and spread of up to 90cm(3ft), its handsome, holly-like pinnaea or leaflets, are glossy dark green and most attractive. They will survive near-freezing temperatures, and are occasionally seen growing outdoors in sheltered sites. A well-drained potting compost, enriched with a little rotted manure, is best; shade them from

Opposite: Asparagus ferns need plenty of room for their attractive arching or trailing foliage to be displayed; they are not true ferns, but members of the lily family.
Right: A young Cyrtomium falcatum, or holly-leaf fern; eventually it forms a substantial, wide-spreading plant.

direct sunlight and water frequently during the growing season and mist occasionally with a fine spray of water if the atmosphere gets too dry. *C.f.* 'Rochfordii' is a compact form.

Davallia canariensis

There are two species of hare's-foot fern which are suitable for indoor growing. The smaller of the two is *D. mariesii*, with 15cm(6in) high greyish-green fronds. These fronds appear at intervals from the thick creeping rhizomes, or surface roots; the rhizomes are covered in furry brown scales which make it resemble an animal's foot and gives the plant its common name. *D. canariensis* is larger, reaching a height and spread of 45cm(18in). Both varieties are deciduous and should be kept nearly dry during the resting season; in spring and summer water freely. In their native habitats they are epiphytic, growing on tree branches; when grown in pots a free-draining, peaty compost is essential. Although *D. mariesii* is occasionally attempted outdoors, both species like a minimum temperature of 10°C(50°F). Propagate from spores, or by division of larger plants in spring.

Nephrolepis

There are over 40 species of *Nephrolepis*, or ladder ferns, as they are sometimes called, but very few of

these are commonly cultivated. The ones that are available, though, are first-class ferns, relatively easy to grow and exceedingly attractive. Perhaps the most popular is *N. bostoniensis*, the Boston fern. The finely divided drooping fronds can be up to 1m (3ft) long, and are best displayed in a hanging basket. *N. exaltata*, the sword fern, grows even larger, with fronds up to 1.5m (5ft) in length. In Victorian times they were often grown on pedestals, with the drooping fronds completely hiding the pots. Nowadays they are rarely seen, perhaps because rooms tend to be much smaller and it is more difficult to accommodate such a large-scale plant. *N.cordifolia* has quite compact fronds, usually no more than 30cm (1ft) long, and is suitable for quite small rooms. All members of this family need protection from direct sunlight, plenty of water in spring and summer and a moderate supply of water during the dormant season. A mimimum temperature of 13°C (55°F) is needed and propagation is from spores or division of plants in spring.

Pellaea rotundifolia

There are several varieties of cliff-brake fern, but *P. rotundifolia* is the one most often grown as a pot plant. From the mountains of New Zealand, it is a compact plant, with a height and spread of 15-30cm (6-12in). Pairs of round pinnaea, or leaflets, are borne all along the length of the dark wiry stems, which arch gracefully from a central crown. Unlike most other ferns, which thoroughly enjoy a moist atmosphere, *Pellaea* has tiny hairs on the underside of the pinnaea which would trap water and encourage rot to set in. Consequently, this plant should be kept in a fairly dry atmosphere. A well-drained growing medium, a shady situation, and a minimum temperature of 7°C (45°F) are needed; propagation is from spores or division.

Platycerium bifurcatum

Although it could hardly be called beautiful in the conventional sense, the stagshorn fern is visually striking and a fascinating subject to grow. In its native Australia, this fern lives on trees and it is often seen in cultivation attached to a piece of bark, with its roots wrapped in sphagnum moss, and held in place with wire. The mid-green fronds can grow to 60cm (2ft) in length, and their resemblance to stag's horns has given the plant its common name. Curiously, the plant has a second set of fronds, which are round in shape and undivided; these lie close to the base of the plant and never bear spores. Stag's horn ferns are excellent subjects for hanging baskets and they do equally well in pots. The key to growing them is absolutely perfect drainage; plenty

of peat and sphagnum moss should be added to a loam-based compost. Top-dress every spring with a mixture of peat, sphagnum moss and bone meal. It is essential that stag's head ferns receive heavy, regular watering during spring and summer; in really hot weather, daily misting is advisable. They should never be exposed to direct sunlight, or a temperature lower than 7°C (45°F). Propagate from spores, or by detaching the young plants which are formed on stolons at the base of the plant.

Pteris

The brake ferns are among the most popular of indoor ferns; this is probably due to the combination of their beauty and the fact that they are almost impossible to kill. They thrive in a wide range of growing conditions, yet appear delicate and fragile without any of the stolidness of an aspidistra. The Victorians adored them, but many of the named varieties which they cultivated have long since disappeared. Most of the ones grown today are derived from *Pteris cretica*, the Cretan brake, which ranges in height from 30-90cm (1-3ft).

The deeply divided pinnaea, or leaflets, are formed at the top of long stems; there are varieties available with white, silver or gold variegation and others have very decorative crests on the ends of the pinnaea. Unlike most ferns, *Pteris cretica* will grow in either sun or shade, although if heavily variegated they should be shielded from direct sunlight, which tends to scorch the leaflets. Use a compost composed of loam, leafmould, peat and sand; water frequently during the growing season and moderately the rest of the year. Propagate from spores or division.

Selaginella

Like the asparagus fern, selaginella is not really a fern at all. However, as it looks like a fern and its cultural requirements are exactly the same as for ferns, it is included in this section. The growth is delicate, dense and moss-like, ranging in height from 15-60cm (6-24in). The most popular variety, *S. martensii*, grows about 30cm (1ft) high and can be had with green or silver-variegated foliage. All selaginellas should be shaded from the sun and given moist, but not stagnant, growing conditions; gritty loams with plenty of peat and sphagnum moss added are best. They should be watered freely during the growing season and misted daily in really hot weather. The one drawback with selaginella is the vigour with which it spreads; for this reason they are best grown on their own, and not mixed with other plants. They are also able to withstand quite cold temperatures, as long as they are protected from frost and are easily propagated from cuttings.

CACTI AND SUCCULENTS

Among cacti and succulents are found many diverse and fascinating plants, all with particular forms of growth which have developed in response to their environments. Most of these plants originate from harsh desert or semi-desert areas where there are long periods of drought only sporadically interrupted with short sharp rainfall.

In order to survive in these conditions, they need to be able to store water for use during the dry periods. 'Succulent' refers to the plant's juicy tissue, either in the stem or leaves, where this water is stored. Besides being able to store water, most cacti and succulents have the ability to reduce the transpiration rate, that is, the loss of water, through the leaves and stems. Some are covered with a waxy coating, others have no leaves at all and the stems act as modifed leaves; a covering of hairs or spines also helps reduce water loss.

There is a certain amount of confusion between the terms 'cactus' and 'succulent'. All cacti are succulents but not all succulents are cacti. *Cactaceae* is the family of plants to which cacti belong, all having similar characteristics of flowering parts. Succulents, however, belong to other families besides *Cactaceae*. Unfortunately, not all cacti flower when grown in cultivation, but there is another tell-tale characteristic which identifies a cactus. This is the presence of areoles, which are small tufted cushions of hair or woolly growth out of which the spines appear. Not all cacti have spines, however; the Christmas and Easter cacti are completely spineless and many spiny succulent plants, such as crown-of-thorns, are not even vaguely related to cacti.

The difficulties in acquiring cacti and succulents have long been overcome and one can now purchase a wide variety of these plants, which are mainly South African or Central or South American in origin, from almost any flower shop or garden centre. Although they are indigenous to many different countries, general advice about their cultivation is applicable to most. The secret of successful growing lies in watering technique; when and when not to water is almost more important than how much water to give. Most true cacti require no water from the end of their growing season in the autumn until the following spring, during which time they should be kept in cool, light conditions. The exception to this rule are tropical-forest cacti, such as *Schlumbergera* and *Zygocactus*, which never dry out totally in their native environments.

Submitting cacti to what may seem excessively harsh treatment not only results in healthy, long-lived plants, it also enables the plants to flower more freely the following season and encourages the production of spines and waxy bloom, qualities for which cacti are grown. When watering cacti and succulents, it is advisable to give the plants a thorough soaking each time the plant is watered, rather than giving small amounts of water at frequent intervals. A free-draining potting mixture is equally important, as stagnant water either in or on the surface of the compost will quickly lead to rot.

Some larger-leaved succulents may require potting on into larger pots as they grow, but on the whole it is best to keep the plants relatively potbound.

Most cacti and succulents grown indoors need the maximum amount of light available; the exceptions are epiphytic forest cacti. Allow plenty of air to circulate around the plants, but keep them out of draughts. As a general rule, temperatures in the region of 15°C (60°F) are suitable for the growing season, and slightly lower temperatures when plants are resting in winter.

Aeonium

These succulents form attractive rosettes of leaves on tall stems and branches, rather like miniature trees. As a rule, bright yellow flowers are produced on the tips of the branches, although one variety, *Aeonium urbicum* has pink flowers. The variety most often grown is *A. domesticum variegatum* which forms a compact plant with round cream and green leaves. If you have plenty of space, *A. arboreum* is worth trying; it grows 1m (3ft) high and produces huge racemes of yellow flowers. Aeoniums tend to get straggly after a while; correct this by pruning back hard any time of the year. The stumps will send out new growth and the cuttings will root quite easily and produce new plants. Aeoniums are easy plants to grow; plenty of light, modest temperature and fairly dry root conditions are the main cultural requirements.

Aporocactus flagelliformis, or rat's tail cactus, gets its rather unfortunate common name from the hanging, cylindrical stems; its deep pink flowers, though, are most attractive.

Aporocactus flagelliformis

This is the popular rat's tail cactus, so called because the spiny, cylindrical stems hang down naturally from the container in which the plants are growing. For this reason, this is a popular plant for hanging baskets. Occasionally it is grafted onto an erect-growing cactus so the stems have room to hang down without trailing over the sides of the pot. Brilliant carmine flowers are produced all along the stem in late spring when the blossoms open during the day and close at night. The rat's tail cactus is a trouble-free plant which thrives in any ordinary growing conditions, provided the soil is rich and free draining. New plants may be raised from seed or pieces of stem which are allowed to dry before inserting in a sandy mixture.

Astrophytum myriostigma

The bishop's hat cactus gets its common name from its geometrical, four-sided squat habit of growth, which resembles a bishop's mitre. This plant eventually reaches a height of 15cm (6in) and needs cool growing conditions and drought during the winter months to produce its large yellow flowers in spring. It is quite attractive even when not in flower, as the spineless surface of the cactus is almost completely covered with small white scales which give the plant a pale grey, speckled appearance. The bishop's hat cactus rarely produces offsets at the base, but is easily propagated from seed.

Cephalocereus senilis

An upright cylindrical cactus with an almost painfully slow rate of growth, the old man cactus is nevertheless a most distinctive plant and worth a place in any collection. Its common name derives from the long, flowing, hair-like bristles which completely cover the stem. The flowers, which are produced at the top of the stem, are almost completely hidden by the hair. Care must be taken when watering, as the old man cactus will rot at the base if conditions are too wet.

Cereus peruvianus

This upright, cylindrical cactus is armed with sharp spines and is one of the easiest cacti to cultivate, although it rarely flowers when grown in pots.

Some species of *Cereus* reach a height of 9m (30ft) or more in their native South America but in cultivation they rarely exceed 1m (3ft) in height. The flowers, which are white and red, appear only on large plants and open only at night. No special care is needed and it can be stood indoors in a sunny position during the summer months. Propagation is from seed or cuttings inserted into sandy compost.

Cephalocereus senilis, or old-man cactus, is grown solely for its display of long, silky white hairs; it is very slow-growing and its flowers are insignificant.

Crassula falcata

This South African succulent is sometimes sold under the name *Rochea falcata*. A shrubby plant, its principal attractions are the bright scarlet flowers and fleshy grey leaves. It grows up to 60cm (2ft) high and should be pruned back if it gets too leggy. The flower heads, which are up to 7.5cm (3in) in diameter, are produced in summer. After flowering, reduce the amount of water given to allow the plant to rest. A sharp, well-drained potting mixture is best, with plenty of grit added. Propagation is from leaf cuttings; allow them to dry out for a day or so before inserting in a sandy compost.

Echeveria

This family contains over 200 species of indoor plants and these are grown largely for the beauty of their rosettes of leaves. The leaves, which have a waxy covering, come in a wide range of colours, depending on the species. Those coloured metallic grey are particularly beautiful. Echeverias need

115

exposure to full sun for well developed leaf colour and to help keep the rosettes compact.

The red or yellow bell-shaped flowers are produced on arching stems and appear in summer and autumn. Echeverias eventually form large carpets of rosettes which can be divided and each piece used to make a new plant. They can also be propagated by leaf or stem cuttings.

Echeverias are quite easy to grow as long as you keep in mind a few simple rules. Avoid getting water on the leaves, because the attractive waxy coating will become disfigured and avoid touching the leaves for the same reason. Give them plenty of sunlight and put the pots outdoors in a sunny sheltered site during the summer months. Water liberally during summer and sparingly the rest of the year. Occasionally, echeverias get somewhat leggy during the winter and lose their bottom leaves. To remedy the situation, cut the tops off in early spring. These rosettes can be planted in sandy compost after drying out for a couple of days. The rosettes will quickly take root and the stumps should also send out new growth.

Echinocactus grusonii

Mature plants of the golden barrel cactus hold pride of place in many collections. Although it may eventually reach a diameter of 1m (3ft) or more, it is very slow growing and can stay quite happily in the same pot for several years. The plant is globe shaped, ribbed and covered with rows of pale yellow spines. Given sufficient heat and light and a winter resting period, a circle of yellow flowers will form on the top of the stem in late spring. Propagation is from seed.

Epiphyllum

Although the flattened, leaf-like stems are not particularly attractive, epiphyllums are spectacular when in flower. The large, bell-shaped blossoms can be up to 12.5cm (5in) across and are usually red, white or yellow in colour. Large numbers of flowers are produced along the stems and they appear over a two-month period in summer.

Most plants sold today under the name epiphyllum are the results of complex hybridization and not really epiphyllums at all. The wild species are found growing on the forest floor in tropical America and, unlike most other cacti, they and their hybrids need a little shade and a continual supply of moisture. Water generously when the buds begin to show: When flowering is over reduce the supply of water for about two months to allow the plants to rest but spray with tepid water to keep the leaves from shrivelling up. In winter, water once every two weeks.

Epiphyllums can be absolutely spectacular when in flower; the blooms, up to 15cm (6in) across, come in a wide range of colours and are very long lasting. The flowers are produced all along the flattened, leaf-like stems.

Epiphyllums can be quite easily propagated from leaf cuttings; allow them to dry for a day or so before inserting them in a sandy compost. Older plants may become untidy in time and can be cut back any time except when they are in flower. Epiphyllums appreciate a rich, peaty compost and regular applications of liquid fertilizer during the growing season.

Euphorbia splendens

This semi-succulent shrub is sometimes sold under the name of *Euphorbia milii*; its common name, crown of thorns, is derived from the fierce thorns which cover the branches. The leaves are small, light green and leathery and attractive red, flower-like bracts usually appear in winter at the bases of the insignificant flowers. Crown-of-thorns grows well in any light, airy and reasonably warm location but be careful not to over-water. The plant is particularly vulnerable to mealy bug infestation. Older specimens tend to have very tightly interwoven branches and mealy bug can prove difficult to eradicate; treat as soon as the first symptoms are seen.

All members of the Euphorbia family ooze a milky sap when cut and when cuttings are taken for propagation purposes it is essential that they should be completely dried before being inserted into a sandy compost. Summer is the best time to take cuttings. Use 10cm (4in) long tips and put several around the edge of a small pot.

Kalanchoe

Although there are over 200 species of kalanchoe, relatively few are widely available. Of these, perhaps the most popular is *K. blossfeldianum*, the florist's kalanchoe. The clusters of tubular, bright red flowers appear from late winter through spring although yellow, pink and white-flowered forms are available as a result of extensive hybridization. The flowers are carried on stems above the bushy, light-green, fleshy leaves; in time, the plant will reach a height and spread of 37cm (15in). They do best in full sun and relatively warm conditions. Water generously in summer and just enough to keep the leaves from shrivelling up in winter. To keep the plant compact, cut back after flowering. New plants can be raised from seed or cuttings; avoid overwatering seedlings and allow cuttings to dry off before inserting them in a sandy compost.

Two other kalanchoes normally acquired as gift plants are *K. tubiflorum* and *K. daigremontianum*; both of these are sometimes sold as *bryophyllums*. These produce perfectly shaped miniature plants on the edges of the leaves. These eventually drop from the leaves and will quickly root in suitable conditions. When the plants become tall and untidy, they should be discarded and replaced with young plants.

Mammillaria

There are more than 200 species of mammillaria and many of these cacti are popular house plants. They have a number of admirable qualities: mammillaria are very easy to grow and propagate, neat and compact in habit and so take up little space and produce showy rings of flowers while still quite young. The best known is probably *M. gracilis* which has a bright green, branching habit of growth and white flowers in summer. The spines lie almost flat against the stem which make a delicate net-like pattern. *M. bocasana* is a very attractive plant, with clusters of pale-green globular stems which are covered with fishhook spines. Pale yellow flowers appear in early summer, followed by violet berries. *M. erythrosperma* is only 5cm (2in) high but eventually forms wide-spreading cushions of spine-covered globular stems. Rose-coloured flowers appear in summer and are followed by small red fruits.

Cultivation is absolutely minimal; keep the plants dry in winter and water them generously in summer. As with most cacti, mamillarias are very vulnerable to excessive water and will simply rot away at the base if over-watered. Make sure the growing compost is free draining so that water does not collect on the surface. A sunny site is best and they can be put outside during the summer months to receive full exposure to sunlight. Bring them in again in early autumn. Propagation is by seed or division of clusters in spring or summer.

Notocactus

By adhering to the general policy of keeping cacti bone dry during the winter months, these relatively small plants can be encouraged to produce enormous, brilliantly coloured flowers in spring. There are fifteen species of notocactus most of which have yellow flowers, although *N. haselbergii* produces bright red flowers and *N. cocinnus* has flowers which are red outside and light yellow inside. All notocactus are typically cactus-shaped, either columnar or globular in habit. No special care is needed provided plenty of light, fresh air and reasonable warmth are given but guard against over-watering. Propagation is from seed or by dividing up the clumps. Most notocactus flower when quite young and produce seed easily, but *N. leninghausii*, which is painfully slow growing, only produces flowers when fully mature. It is, however, a most beautiful cactus, with golden yellow, fat, cylindrical growth, and well worth having.

Opuntia

This plant, commonly called the prickly pear cactus, is one of the most familiar cacti; no western epic seems complete without prickly pears forming part of the landscape. In fact, opuntia is an enormous genus, with species varying widely in appearance and size; the sub-genus *Platyopuntia* contains most of the typical prickly-pears, with flattened, pad-like stems. Each of these pads grows from the tip of another pad; the removal of these sections as they mature makes propagation a simple business. These are quite vigorous and in time will develop into plants of considerable size. They can, however, be kept in check simply by cutting them back. Unfortunately, most opuntias flower only when they have reached full size, but many are attractive enough in form to be grown for their shape alone. *Opuntia scheeri* is a popular species; in cultivation it eventually reaches a height of 1m (3ft) and its deep-green, oval pads are covered with yellow spines and light yellow hairs. *Opuntia microdasys* is another commonly grown prickly-pear cactus. It has no spines, but the glaucous oval pads are conspicuously dotted with small golden tufts. *O.m. rufida* has red tufts of tiny barbed hairs and there is a form with white tufts.

Parodia

These compact globular cacti are covered with vicious hooked spines which present an impenetrable defence. They are most attractive and intriguing plants, however, and produce brilliantly-coloured flowers early in the year. *P. chrysacanthion*, which is pale green, has bright yellow flowers; *P. sanguini-flora*, as its name suggests, has deep red flowers and are easy to cultivate; give full light and plenty of water in the growing season.

Rebutia

These relatively small globular cacti are unusual in that they produce flowers from areoles at the base of the plant rather than at the top. The flowers are long-lasting, spectacular and are carried on quite young plants. It is an easy cactus to cultivate and well worth having in any collection. Most rebutias produce off-sets and eventually form cushions; these offsets can be divided up and repotted in summer if new plants are wanted. They are also easily raised from seed and require no special treatment except protection from direct sunlight. South American in origin, rebutias need plenty of leaf mould in the growing medium, plus a little sand for free drainage. Water sparingly at all times, particularly in winter.

There are more than fifty species of rebutia, but only a dozen or so are commonly available. Of these, the most popular are *R. deminuta* and *R. senilis*, with bright red flowers, *R. aureiflora* and *R. marsoneri* with bright yellow flowers and *R. xanthocarpa* with a wide variety of flower colours.

Schlumbergera gaertneri

Better known as Easter cactus, schlumbergera is a household favourite and a popular gift plant. Al-

though a member of the cactus family, it is quite different from most other cacti in appearance and cultivation. The plants are spineless and the leaf-like pads that make up the plant are really flattened stems. Bright, tubular, star-like flowers, in various shades of pink or red, appear at the tips of the stems in spring. Although each flower only lasts for a few days, many flowers are produced and the plant is quite spectacular when in bloom. A word of warning: Easter cactus will shed its blossom if subjected to extreme changes in temperature, moisture or growing conditions, so disturb it as little as possible when it is flowering.

Natives of South America, schlumbergeras are forest cacti and should not be exposed to direct sunlight. They can be stood outdoors in light shade during the summer months to ripen growth; in winter keep the temperature above 13°C (55°F). Grow in a compost which has plenty of leaf mould and sand added and feed regularly with liquid manure when the flower buds form. Water moderately in autumn and winter and generously the rest of the year. Propagation is from cuttings of the leaf-like pads once flowering has finished.

Senecio articulata

This is the candle plant, which is also sold under the name *Kleinia articulata*. The succulent, cylindrical stems are pale grey and covered with a waxy bloom. It has a curious habit of growth; in winter new stems are formed on the tips of existing stems. Although small, pale-green leaves and inconspicuous flowers are produced, it is really the stick-like, joined stems perched one on top of another which make the plant popular. It is very easily propagated; parts of stem broken off and dibbed into almost any mixture will quickly take root.

Sedum

There are many hardy plants in this genus, including the popular stonecrops. The tender species are usually Mexican in origin, although one or two are Japanese. They vary enormously in appearance but all thrive in full sun and poor soil with plenty of sharp sand added. *Sedum morganianum*, commonly called burro's tail, has pendulous stems of tightly packed pale-green leaves. It is an excellent plant for a hanging basket as it has light pink flowers are produced at the tips of the stems in summer. *Sedum rubrotinctum* has small, bead-like leaves on slender stems; although attractive, it can become a nuisance as the leaves fall off and produce new plants almost anywhere. *Sedum seiboldii* is hardy enough to be grown outdoors in mild sheltered sites but also makes an attractive indoor plant. The pendant stems are deciduous and clusters of round, flat grey leaves appear in early spring, followed by pink flowers in autumn. *S.s. Mediovariegatum* has attractive yellow colouration in the centres of the leaves.

Keep the plants in a minimum temperature of 10°C (50°F) in winter and water when the stems begin to shrivel.

Stapelia

This succulent is one of the more difficult plants to grow but many people find the fleshy, star-shaped brown or purple and yellow flowers attractive and worth the extra effort. Its common name, carrion flower, refers to the putrid odour emitted by the open blossom; the odour attracts blowflies which then pollinate the flowers.

Although there are about one hundred species of carrion flower, only a few are available commercially. They all have fleshy, four-angled stems. New stems are produced from the base of the plant and in time the older centre of the plant will die. The flowers appear at the base of the stems in late summer and if pollination is successful, seed pods form which later burst open to release the seeds. An open, sandy compost with a little old mortar is best, and a position in full sunlight. Water moderately in spring and summer and very sparingly the rest of the year. Carrion flowers are very vulnerable to excessive water and will quickly rot in wet conditions.

The easiest carrion flower to cultivate is *S. hirsuta*, which grows about 20cm (8in) high and has large yellow flowers which are striped reddish brown. *S. variegata* is perhaps the most popular, growing to a height of 10cm (4in) and producing deep yellow and purple flowers. Unfortunately, it has a particularly offensive odour.

Zygocactus truncatus

This plant is very similar in appearance to the Easter cactus and is sometimes included in the genus *Schlumbergera*. Its common name, Christmas cactus‘ refers to the time of the year that the deep-rosê coloured flowers are produced, although it can flower any time from December through to February. Sometimes, quite inexplicably, it will fail to flower at all and this may be due to too much water or insufficient heat or light. Cultivation and propagation is as for *Schlumbergera*.

Opposite: the flowers of stapelia are more fascinating than beautiful and their fragrance is definitely unpleasant, but many people enjoy the challenge involved in growing them successfully. South African in origin, they need full light, warmth and careful watering, as excessive watering will cause rot to set in.

Right: Zygocactus truncatus, or Christmas cactus, is probably one of the most popular of succulents. This is due to the cheerful, longlasting floral display in winter and the ease of propagation; leaf cuttings quickly root and a healthy specimen can be an infinite source of new plants for distribution among friends and neighbours.

119

INDEX